T0160595

the GAME OF LIFE WORKBOOK

FLORENCE SCOVEL SHINN'S PROSPERITY CLASSIC
NEWLY EXPANDED WITH LIFE-CHANGING EXERCISES AND TOOLS

BY KATE LARGE

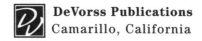

DeVorss Publications
Camarillo, California

THE GAME OF LIFE WORKBOOK
Copyright © 2013 by Kate Large

ISBN: 9780875168692
SECOND PRINTING, 2016

DeVorss & Company, Publisher
PO Box 1389
Camarillo CA 93011-1389
www.devorss.com

Printed in the United States of America.

Table of Contents

■ ■ ■ ■ ■

Acknowledgments

■ ■ ■ ■ ■

Life has been an exciting adventure — the teachers have come and gone in miraculous ways.

Thank you to Sherry Lewis who introduced me to Florence Scovel Shinn's work. Sherry loaned me her copy of *The Game of Life* and I never gave it back. As a matter of fact, I cut the spine off the book, hole-punched the pages and put them into a notebook to access easily when I wrote the e-course, *The Keys to Unlocking the Secrets – The Game of Life Unleashed!*

Thank you to Barbara Mark who gave me the title for the original e-course. Barbara suggested the title from the spirit world where she now resides and continues to bring love and laughter to my life.

Thank you to Jennifer Hoffman for being the beautiful, loving, nonjudgmental, supportive essence that you are. When asked if she thought I could do something, she didn't hesitate, she firmly answered with all the authority that *is* Jennifer, "Of course you can!"

Thank you to those of you who experienced the e-course and loved it!

Thank you to those of you who are experiencing this workbook! May your lives shift to prosperous abundance and joy.

I also want to thank my husband, Fred Winther, for his generous support during the thousands of hours spent working with Florence.

Introduction

■ ■ ■ ■ ■

The Game of Life, by Florence Scovel Shinn, came to me during a very sad, unhappy period of time in my life. I had foolishly given my personal power away and it felt as if my life force was draining from me. Then a miracle occurred. I met a wonderful woman who saw the light of God shining within me trying so desperately to survive the physical world. She asked the angels what she could do to help me and they led her to her bookcase. As she stood there in front of the books, she asked which one to loan to me. *The Game of Life and How to Play It,* by Florence Scovel Shinn, fell to the floor.

As I read the words of wisdom Florence shared in the book, I couldn't put it down. What Florence had written so many years before resonated deep within me. I took back my personal power and began to search within for my true self and reconnect with the Divinity within. As God's voice spoke in my heart, my spiritual journey began.

Many of us float around on the sea of life aimlessly drifting, living our lives from an unconscious lower energy state of fear. Then one day it's as if we wake up and realize we're unhappy with the life we've created. We want something different. So as we try to create a new life — using the same old patterns and thought processes — we end up creating more of what we don't want and feeling worse. Do you see the problem? Albert Einstein understood this disappointing reality when he said:

"We can't solve problems by using the same kind of thinking we used when we created them."

You've opened this workbook because on some level (conscious or not) you wish to change your life to be something different. *The Game of Life Workbook* explores your current "same kind of thinking" to help you stimulate and shift thought patterns into a new WAY of thinking that ignites the enlightenment and transformation you seek. It brings 1925 terminology into the twenty-first century to guide you to reconnect with the essence of who you are: a limitless spiritual being of infinite possibility.

The Game of Life Workbook is a powerful tool that will only "click" with people when they are ready. Florence's work is timeless and magical in the sense that each time it is read, new insight and empowerment are discovered, because with each reading the reader is at a higher level of consciousness.

The teachings that Florence gave us in *The Game of Life* are based on the belief that the energy of our thoughts creates our reality. She uses real-life examples to explain the cause and effect of trusting in God as our supply. Using her examples, this workbook delves deeply into her words and offers tools and experiential exercises to understand and attain a higher level of love consciousness. The exercises light the way to implement Florence's teachings to help us shift from the bondage of fear in our "Normal" way of living to a "New Normal" in the healed energy of love as a prosperity magnet!

Make no mistake — after experiencing *The Game of Life Workbook* your life will change forever and you will never be able to go back to simply existing in the conditioned life you were living. You will be empowered by your connection with God and the understanding of Universal Laws. You will tap the unlimited depths of your spiritual being-ness and learn how to release the old (conditioned) thought patterns and illuminate the path to a life of infinite possibilities.

REPETITION WITH PURPOSE

Florence was "before her time" in a multitude of ways. She had a special gift of teaching a concept from different perspectives in order to reach "understanding of the masses." This seeming repetition reveals the depth of the subject matter, yet may be interpreted by some simply as repetition. Don't be fooled. The magic of this style of teaching allows the student to achieve a much deeper level of understanding each time the subject is approached. The workbook, written with Florence's guidance, follows suit with "repetition with purpose."

We are beings of conditioned layers of fear. As we evolve and grow a new layer of fear is revealed to us. The work of Florence Scovel Shinn helps us peel back these layers, resolve, heal, and dissipate the fear, thereby ascending in our transformation of mind, body, and spirit. With each chapter and workbook session of *The Game of Life Workbook* we uncover new layers.

This is an *interactive* workbook. Take the time you need to work through each session. The journaling is an extremely valuable tool. Take a few minutes to write about your experience. This step is as important as the processes of the workbook. As you work your way through the workbook, refer back to the experiences of the previous exercises. The concepts that were perhaps a little confusing will become clearer as the journaling helps you to anchor the energy shift to your "New Normal." *Don't skip the journaling — you will be cheating yourself if you do!*

Once you've completed the *The Game of Life Workbook*, go back from time to time and experience the workbook again — you will be amazed at how *much more* you will learn, understand, and experience. Each time the workbook is opened, new growth and ascension is discovered.

It's time to say good-bye to the "Normal" life of lack and limitation laced with fear that you have been living. In the blank below, write your name and start claiming a new life of infinite possibilities.

I,_____, now set and anchor my intention to heal the fear within me and reconnect with my Higher Self. I now prepare myself to receive all that is mine by Divine Right, under grace, in a miraculous way.

Who Was (Is) Florence Scovel Shinn?

■ ■ ■ ■ ■

Florence Scovel Shinn was an artist, actress, and metaphysical teacher who began touching people's lives in miraculous ways in the 1920s. She learned to tap into the source of human existence, reconnecting as One with God. She understood how and why people created fearful, unhappy lives that spiraled out of control, and held the space for them to make the changes necessary to create a life of love and happiness.

As noted in the introductory essay to *The Writings of Florence Scovel Shinn* by Arthur Vergara, Florence's "game of life" began with her birth on September 24, 1871. Her American blue blood family members included a signatory to the Declaration of Independence, a member of the team who designed the American flag, and a "Mayflower Biddle" who was related to George Washington.

Florence studied art at the Pennsylvania Academy of Fine Arts, where she met and married Everett Shinn. While they were married, she continued with art, added acting to her repertoire, and became well known for her "brilliant conversation and quick wit." After fourteen years of marriage, Florence and Everett divorced.

The divorce stimulated her new career as a metaphysical teacher and lecturer. Florence was ahead of her time: not only was she a divorced woman in the 1920s, she also questioned organized religion and advocated New Thought ideals of reconnecting with the God Part within. She compiled her teachings in *The Game of Life and How to Play It*, but no publisher would touch it. She published it herself in 1925.

Vergara states, "Unfortunately we have no other accounts of Florence Scovel Shinn in her second flowering [life as a metaphysical teacher], the one that enabled so many thousands themselves to bloom — or, to use her better metaphor, to play the game of life and win at it…We do know that it was in her apartment at 1136 Fifth Avenue that Florence Shinn passed away, a half hour before noon on October 17, 1940, at 69. The attending physician did not indicate the nature of her short illness. [Noted New York writer] Ira Glackens comments:

"Finally one day Flossie went into her living room, sat down and died. Not long afterward her effects were sold in a dingy auction room. E.G. [Edith Glackens, Ira's

*mother]...found Flossie's goods and chattels had been sold
and carted away. Only a few of her old drawings were scattered on the floor, not yet having been swept up, and the
attendant said she might have them. So E., faithful to her
old friend, picked up the drawings off the floor and carried
them home. No one else had cared. One or two of these
rescued drawings are now in the Library of Congress.*

"And on that note the story ends. But not really. Many
thousands more than those Florence Scovel Shinn reached
in person have made her life a very real part of theirs. Is it
too much to suggest that in and through them she continues to play 'the game of life'?"

KNOW THAT FLORENCE HAS NOT LEFT THE BUILDING...

Florence's spirit is alive, well, and very active in the realm
of the fourth dimension. *And* she wants everyone to know
she was never alone. She fully understood the connection
humans have with the angelic realm and she lived her life
path as one with God. She had fully reconnected with the
source of her life force energy and completed her mission
for incarnating to Mother Earth as Florence Scovel Shinn.

Florence Scovel Shinn was and still is a remarkable metaphysical teacher with a true gift of holding the space for us
to look deeply within and face the fears of this lifetime as
well as the fears of past lifetimes. As you work through this
workbook ask yourself, "What would Florence do in this
situation?" Don't be surprised when you receive a sign (or
a "lead," as Florence calls it) to guide you. Florence now
has the ability to be omnipresent and she takes a personal
interest as a guiding light to those who desire to change
their lives to something better through her teachings.

Dedication

■ ■ ■ ■ ■

This workbook is dedicated to Florence Scovel Shinn with deepest gratitude for providing me with guidance and direction to create my version of Heaven on Earth.

CHAPTER 1

The Game

■ ■ ■ ■ ■

Most people consider life a battle, but it is not a battle, it is a game. It is a game, however, which cannot be played successfully without the knowledge of spiritual law, and the Old and the New Testaments give the rules of the game with wonderful clearness. Jesus Christ taught that it was a great game of *Giving and Receiving*.

"Whatsoever a man soweth that shall he also reap." This means that whatever man sends out in word or deed will return to him; what he gives, he will receive.

If he gives hate, he will receive hate; if he gives love, he will receive love; if he gives criticism, he will receive criticism; if he lies, he will be lied to; if he cheats, he will be cheated. We are taught also that the imaging faculty plays a leading part in the game of life.

"Keep thy heart (or imagination) with all diligence, for out of it are the issues of life." (Prov. 4:23)

This means that what man images, sooner or later externalizes in his affairs. I know of a man who feared a certain disease. It was a very rare disease and difficult to get, but he pictured it continually and read about it until it manifested in his body, and he died, the victim of distorted imagination.

So we see, to successfully play the game of life, we must train the imaging faculty. A person with an imaging faculty trained to image only good, brings into his life "every righteous desire of his heart" — health, wealth, love, friends, perfect self-expression, his highest ideals.

————————————

————————————

————————————

————————————

————————————

————————————

————————————

————————————

————————————

————————————

————————————

————————————

————————————

————————————

The imagination has been called *"The Scissors of the Mind,"* and it is ever cutting, cutting, day by day, the pictures man sees there, and sooner or later he meets his own creations in his outer world. To train the imagination successfully, man must understand the workings of his mind. The Greeks said: "Know Thyself."

There are three departments of the mind, the *subconscious, conscious,* and *superconscious.* The subconscious is simply power, without direction. It is like steam or electricity, and it does what it is directed to do; it has no power of induction.

Whatever man feels deeply or images clearly is impressed upon the subconscious mind, and carried out in the minutest detail.

For example: a woman I know, when a child, always "made believe" she was a widow. She "dressed up" in black clothes and wore a long black veil, and people thought she was very clever and amusing. She grew up and married a man with whom she was deeply in love. In a short time he died and she wore black and a sweeping veil for many years. The picture of herself as a widow was impressed upon the subconscious mind, and in due time worked itself out, regardless of the havoc created.

The conscious mind has been called mortal or carnal mind.

It is the human mind and sees life as it *appears to be.* It sees death, disaster, sickness, poverty, and limitation of every kind, and it impresses the subconscious.

The *superconscious* mind is the God Mind within each man, and is the realm of perfect ideas.

In it is the *"perfect pattern"* spoken of by Plato, *The Divine Design;* for there is a *Divine Design* for each person.

"There is a place that you are to fill and no one else can fill, something you are to do, which no one else can do."

There is a perfect picture of this in the *superconscious* mind. It usually flashes across the conscious as an unattainable ideal — something too good to be true.

In reality it is man's true destiny (or destination) flashed to him from the Infinite Intelligence that is *within himself.*

Many people, however, are in ignorance of their true destinies and are striving for things and situations that do not belong to them, and would only bring failure and dissatisfaction if attained.

For example: A woman came to me and asked me to "speak the word" that she would marry a certain man with whom she was very much in love. (She called him A. B.)

I replied that this would be a violation of spiritual law, but that I would speak the word for the right man, the "divine selection," the man who belonged to her by Divine Right.

I added, "If A. B. is the right man you can't lose him, and if he isn't, you will receive his equivalent." She saw A. B. frequently but no headway was made in their friendship. One evening she called and said, "Do you know, for the last week, A. B. hasn't seemed so wonderful to me." I replied, "Maybe he is not the divine selection — another man may be the right one." Soon after that, she met another man who fell in love with her at once, and who said she was his ideal. In fact, he said all the things that she had always wished A. B. would say to her.

She remarked, "It was quite uncanny."

She soon returned his love, and lost all interest in A. B.

This shows the law of substitution. A right idea was substituted for a wrong one, therefore there was no loss or sacrifice involved.

Jesus Christ said, "Seek ye first the kingdom of God and his righteousness; and all these things shall be added unto you," and he said the Kingdom *was within man*.

The Kingdom is the realm of *right ideas*, or the divine pattern.

Jesus Christ taught that man's words played a leading part in the game of life. "By your words ye are justified and by your words ye are condemned."

Many people have brought disaster into their lives through idle words.

For example: A woman once asked me why her life was now one of poverty of limitation. Formerly she had a home, was surrounded by beautiful things and had often tired of the management of her home, and had said repeatedly, "I'm sick and tired of things — I wish I lived in a trunk," and she added: "Today I am living in that trunk." She had spoken herself into a trunk. The subconscious mind has no sense of humor and people often joke themselves into unhappy experiences.

For example: A woman who had a great deal of money, joked continually about "getting ready for the poorhouse."

In a few years she was almost destitute, having impressed the subconscious mind with a picture of lack and limitation.

———————————————

———————————————

———————————————

———————————————

———————————————

———————————————

———————————————

———————————————

———————————————

———————————————

———————————————

———————————————

———————————————

———————————————

Fortunately the law works both ways, and a situation of lack may be changed to one of plenty.

For example: A woman came to me one hot summer's day for a "treatment" for prosperity. She was worn out, dejected, and discouraged. She said she possessed just eight dollars in the world. I said, "Good, we'll bless the eight dollars and multiply them as Jesus Christ multiplied the loaves and fishes," for He taught that *every man* had the power to bless and to multiply, to heal and to prosper.

She said, "What shall I do next?"

I replied, "Follow intuition. Have you a 'hunch' to do anything, or to go anywhere?" Intuition means to be taught from within. It is man's unerring guide, and I will deal more fully with its laws in a following chapter.

The woman replied: "I don't know — I seem to have a 'hunch' to go home; I've just enough money for car fare." Her home was in a distant city and was one of lack and limitation, and the reasoning mind (or intellect) would have said: "Stay in New York and get work and make some money." I replied, "Then go home — never violate a hunch." I spoke the following words for her: *Infinite Spirit open the way for great abundance for —. She is an irresistible magnet for all that belongs to her by Divine Right.* I also told her to repeat it continually. She left for home immediately. In calling on a woman one day, she linked up with an old friend of her family.

Through this friend, she received thousands of dollars in a most miraculous way. She has said to me often, "Tell people about the woman who came to you with eight dollars and a hunch."

There is always *plenty on man's pathway*; but it can only be *brought into manifestation* through desire, faith, or the spoken word. Jesus Christ brought out clearly that man must make the *first move.*

"Ask, and it shall be given you, seek, and ye shall find, knock, and it shall be opened unto you." (Mat. 7:7)

In the scriptures we read:

"Concerning the works of my hands, command ye me."

Infinite Intelligence, God, is ever ready to carry out man's smallest or greatest demands.

Every desire, uttered or unexpressed, is a demand. We are often startled by having a wish suddenly fulfilled.

For example: One Easter, having seen many beautiful rose-trees in the florists' windows, I wished I would receive one, and for an instant saw it mentally being carried in the door.

Easter came, and with it a beautiful rose-tree. I thanked my friend the following day, and told her it was just what I had wanted.

She replied, "I didn't send you a rose-tree, I sent you lilies!"

The man had mixed up the order, and sent me a rose-tree simply because I had started the law in action, and *I had to have a rose-tree.*

Nothing stands between man and his highest ideals and every desire of his heart but doubt and fear. When man can "wish without worrying," every desire will be instantly fulfilled.

I will explain more fully in a following chapter the scientific reason for this and how fear must be erased from the consciousness. It is man's only enemy — fear of lack, fear of failure, fear of sickness, fear of loss, and a feeling *of insecurity on some plane.* Jesus Christ said: "Why are ye fearful, oh ye of little faith?" (Mat. 8:26) So we can see we must substitute faith for fear, for fear is only inverted faith; it is faith in evil instead of good.

The object of the game of life is to see clearly one's good and to obliterate all mental pictures of evil. This must be done by impressing the subconscious mind with a realization of good. A very brilliant man, who has attained great success, told me he had suddenly erased all fear from his consciousness by reading a sign that hung in a room. He saw printed, in large letters this statement: "*Why worry, it will probably never happen.*" These words were stamped indelibly upon his subconscious mind, and he has now a firm conviction that only good can come into his life, therefore only *good can manifest.*

In the following chapter I will deal with the different methods of impressing the subconscious mind. It is man's faithful servant but one must be careful to give it the right orders. Man has ever a silent listener at his side — his subconscious mind.

Every thought, every word is impressed upon it and carried out in amazing detail. It is like a singer making a record on the sensitive disc of the phonographic plate. Every note and tone of the singer's voice is registered. If he coughs or hesitates, it is registered also. So let us break all the old bad records in the subconscious mind, the records of our lives that we do not wish to keep, and make new and beautiful ones.

_____

_____

_____

_____

_____

_____

_____

_____

_____

_____

_____

_____

_____

Speak these words aloud, with power and conviction: "I now smash and demolish (by my spoken word) every untrue record in my subconscious mind. They shall return to the dust-heap of their native nothingness, for they came from my own vain imaginings. I now make my perfect records through the Christ within — the records of *Health, Wealth, Love, and Perfect Self-Expression.*" This is the Square of Life, *The Game completed.*

In the following chapters, I will show how man can *change his conditions by changing his words*. Any man who does not know the power of the word, is behind the times.

WORKBOOK SESSION ONE

The Game

Topics:

- The Square of Life
- Thoughts Are Energy
- Three Levels of Consciousness
- The Subconscious Mind
- Identifying and Releasing Feelings of "Not Good Enough"
- The Conscious Mind
- Inner and Outer Voices
- The Shift from Fear to Love
- The Superconscious Mind

- Tapping into the Quiet Voice Within
- The Enemy Is Within — Fear
- Soul Purpose and The New Paradigm
- Divine Life Path
- The Divine Selection/Divine Right
- Field of Potentiality, Birthright, Manifesting Abundance
- Rewriting the Subconscious Records
- Infinite Intelligence — God Is Ever Ready!
- Recap and Personal Journal

We begin each session with a prayer and a few quiet moments to open our mind and heart to the limitless possibilities of our individual spiritual being-ness. Breathe deeply to achieve balance within and surround yourself with God's Divine White Light of Protection, then set your intention to connect with your Higher Self within.

Father, Mother, God, Creator of All That Is…

I claim my personal power and open the way to see clearly my Field of Potentiality, my field of infinite possibilities. I cut the ties of beliefs and thought patterns that no longer serve me in all directions of time, removing them from my consciousness, my subconscious, and my superconscious. I fearlessly step into the magnificence of the true essence of who I am — One with God. I graciously accept all that is mine by Divine Right, under grace in a miraculous way and commit to fulfill all that I came to be, have, and do in this incarnation on Mother Earth at this time.

Amen

Ask your guides, angels, and teachers to be present with you to help you open your heart, mind, and spirit to the infinite possibility that is *YOU*.

The inner workings of Chapter 1, The Game, is loaded with information. Please take your time and allow yourself to fully integrate all that is here before moving on to the next chapter and session.

The object of *The Game of Life* is to see clearly and create your highest good by releasing the mental pictures, thoughts, and beliefs of being limited — all things negative.

Florence teaches that perfect happiness can only be achieved by living in an abundance of prosperity in the Square of Life, four integral aspects of success and prosperity: Health, Wealth, Love, and Perfect Self-Expression. To help you understand how the Square of Life identifies your mental pictures, thoughts and beliefs, I've created a form that we will utilize throughout this book. Below is an example.

HEALTH	WEALTH
I deserve a healthy physical body that houses my spirit	I deserve cash flow that fulfills my needs and desires
LOVE	PERFECT SELF-EXPRESSION
I deserve relationships that are fulfilling and love based	I deserve work that fulfills my passion

THE SQUARE OF LIFE

Florence states that our Square of Life is:

- HEALTH — A healthy physical body that houses our spirit

- WEALTH — Cash flow that fulfills our needs and desires

- LOVE — Relationships that are fulfilling and love based

- PERFECT SELF-EXPRESSION — Work that fulfills our passion

We are magnets for what we continually focus on. If we are truly connected with the Higher Self within us, there will be no fear or doubt in our lives. Love-based thoughts, feelings, and beliefs draw to us our highest good, based in love. Fear-based thoughts, feelings and beliefs draw to us things we do not want, things based in fear. When we live fully from a source of love our thoughts will be "positive" and of our "highest good," making us a magnet for the abundance we desire in the four areas of the Square of Life creating prosperity.

Receiving prosperous abundance is NOT a reward for good behavior. We live in an abundant Universe. We choose with our thoughts and deep-seated beliefs whether we are in an abundance of lack or an abundance of prosperity. Prosperous abundance from the Universe/God is our birthright.

What does your Square of Life look like? Are all areas of your life working? If we honestly evaluate what we continually think of, will we be horrified? Before we look at your personal Square of Life, we need to understand how our thoughts impact our lives.

THOUGHTS ARE ENERGY

"Whatsoever a man soweth that shall he also reap." This is deeper than just actions and words. This includes thoughts as well. Thoughts, actions, and words are powerful. Whatever we send out in word, action, or thought, will return to us.

How can this be?

What we continually think about will manifest as the reality of our lives. If we continually focus on lack, we will always be in an *abundant state of lack*. If we focus, worry, and fret over a specific disease or illness, our body will attract it. If we continually focus on how blessed and prosperous we are, we will live a life of prosperity. If we could see the energy surrounding us that our words and thoughts create, we would be more careful as to the type of energy — positive or negative — that we put out!

Our minds are like a microwave creating energy not only within, but also sending that energy out into the world to manifest the reality of our lives.

Florence uses the example of a man who feared a certain disease. Continually thinking of it caused his energy (his fear) to make him a magnet for the disease, thereby bringing it into his reality.

She states, to "play successfully the game of life (bring what we really want into our lives), we must train the imaging faculty." The imaging faculty is our mind.

Training our mind to bring good into our lives typically doesn't happen on its own. Beginning as babies, we are physically conditioned to fear and limit ourselves. By the time we become teenagers we have developed limiting thought patterns and beliefs. Most of our lives are lived believing in lack, fear, and personal limitations.

Florence states: "Jesus Christ taught that man's words play a leading part in the game of life. 'By your words ye are justified and by your words ye are condemned.'" The first exercise illuminates the shadow thoughts of fear that sabotage your creation energy.

1 ▶ INSIDE ASSIGNMENT

Where Is Your Focus? Where is your focus? What do you spend your time thinking about? Are you fretting or worrying about how you'll pay the rent, mortgage, car payment, credit cards, doctor bills, utilities, how you will put food on the table, your health, or your relationships with family, friends, or co-workers? Are you burdened by how much you hate your job and feel trapped?

When you review your life what thoughts immediately come to mind? Write down the thoughts that hold your focus and cause stress or make you worry about outcomes. Be honest when you write your answers.

Anything negative is fear based. Your thoughts are either of love source or of fear source — there is NO in between!

In order to change your life you must be willing to change the negative thought patterns and beliefs. You must be willing to change the need within you to experience life situations that do not bring you joy.

The thoughts you wrote down identify lower vibrational energies of fear in your daily thought patterns. Do you see the pattern of negative energy in your normal thinking process?

Use the Personal Journal to anchor what you learned about your thoughts.

1. _____

_____

_____

2. _____

_____

_____

3. _____

_____

_____

4. _____

_____

_____

THREE LEVELS OF CONSCIOUSNESS

The true POWER of our mind is governed by three levels of consciousness:

- SUBCONSCIOUS — the soul and essence
- CONSCIOUS — the physical world
- SUPERCONSCIOUS — the Higher Self

THE SUBCONSCIOUS MIND

It is our inner voice where deep-seated beliefs of all things negative and positive of this lifetime and past lifetimes reside. Unfortunately it is the part of the mind with the least supervision. We become magnets for negative things through deep-seated negative energy we aren't even aware we have.

Example: if we have a fear of lack, it lives unchecked in the subconscious mind, making us a magnet for lack. So if we have deep-seated feelings that are positive, such as completely believing we are worthy to receive our highest good, that we are naturally prosperous, then we become a magnet for prosperity.

The subconscious mind works with the superconscious (the Universe) to match the vibrational frequency/energy of what we continually focus on at a subconscious level. Our vibrational frequency attracts people and things of the same vibrational frequency. This is the Law of Attraction.

The Superconscious/Universe holds our Field of Potentiality and is virtually a limitless supply warehouse with more than enough for everyone. There is no lack at this higher plane of existence — only prosperity.

We also must keep in mind that the subconscious mind has NO sense of humor. Florence used the example of the woman who repeatedly said she was getting ready for the poorhouse. The woman was joking, but she became almost destitute. The energy of her words made her a magnet for lack and limitation.

If you are blocked in an area of your Square of Life, unable to create what makes your heart sing with joy, your first step is to look within to identify the negative blocking energy. Discerning the negative deep-seated belief is the key. Negative feelings, such as unworthiness, stem from deep within and many times we are completely unaware of them.

2 ▶ INSIDE ASSIGNMENT

Deep-Seated Beliefs This exercise will be the first step to discerning what your deep-seated beliefs are with regard to fear of lack and feelings of worthiness.

Sit quietly and think about your Square of Life. Think about it honestly. Do you have any deep-seated negative beliefs about yourself? Are you engulfed with fear of lack? When you think about being worthy to receive good things in your life, where do you feel it in your body and what do you feel? Do you feel elated and joyful or do you feel like perhaps you don't deserve good things?

Read each section of the Square of Life and evaluate how you feel when you digest the words. Identify your feelings of worthiness or unworthiness as best you can. As you read each section do you truly feel deep within you that you are worthy to receive prosperity? Write your answers in the section.

Did you find yourself experiencing feelings of unworthiness? Good things in your life are not rewards for good behavior. It is your birthright to receive Prosperous Abundance in your Square of Life. Infinite Spirit, The Creator, Heavenly Father, Mother, God is a loving being who has great abundance for everyone. It is up to you to use your free will wisely and allow yourself to receive what you truly desire.

Feeling worthy to receive prosperous abundance, the birthright of humans, is a challenge for most people. Through physical world conditioning you feel limited in what you can receive, limited in what you can do, limited in what you can be. Know that in God, there are no limits.

Were you surprised at what you learned about the inner workings of your subconscious thoughts? Use the Journal Page to write about what you have discovered.

SQUARE OF LIFE — IDENTIFYING BELIEFS

HEALTH I deserve a healthy physical body that houses my spirit	**WEALTH** I deserve cash flow that fulfills my needs and desires
LOVE I deserve relationships that are fulfilling and love based	**PERFECT SELF-EXPRESSION** I deserve work that fulfills my passion

IDENTIFYING AND RELEASING FEELINGS OF "NOT GOOD ENOUGH"

Beliefs of unworthiness and emotions linked to them are often so deeply seated into the subconscious that they feel "normal"—not foreign or bad. They are a part of us that flies under our radar; therefore it is critical to dig them out!

The root of feelings of unworthiness stems from fear — often it is fear of not being good enough. If we don't like our job, we may stay in the job by telling ourselves we are stuck due to the economy or lack of education. But the truth is FEAR is holding us hostage, fear that we aren't good enough to perform the job we truly desire. This is the Law of Attraction working against us, drawing to us what we don't want because we are vibrating at the lower energy of fear in feeling unworthy.

The reality is that when we are in alignment energetically with what we desire nothing can hold us back. The Universe matches what we desire to us and it manifests into our reality. This is the universal Law of Attraction working for us.

Sometimes we are self-saboteurs. We all do it on occasion, but we have the power to get rid of fear and doubt and allow ourselves to receive God's abundance — all that is ours by Divine Right!

After you have completed the inside assignment, use the Journal Page to write about what you discovered about your feelings of being worthy. Were the words you used to describe your feelings of love source or fear source? Look back at your life, do you see times when you "thought" yourself worthy, then at the last moment became fearful that you weren't. This shift in energy blocked your highest good from coming to you.

A very effective method to release deep-seated negative beliefs and thought patterns is The Sedona Method® of Release, a simple technique that allows you to let go of neg-ative thoughts, feelings, or emotions (printed with permission of Sedona Training Associates, Sedona.com). The procedure will help you release negative beliefs and/or thought patterns that are blocking your receipt of prosperity. Refer to "The Sedona Method® of Release" in the back of the workbook.

3   INSIDE ASSIGNMENT

Are You Worthy? This exercise is designed to help you identify more specifically your true feelings of worthiness to receive the prosperous abundance that is your birthright. You will identify negative feelings, thought patterns, and beliefs and rid yourself of them.

Read the heading of each section of the Square of Life Form. Look deeply within and identify what you feel: joy, happiness, elation, worry, anxiety, fear, etc. Write down a one-word summary of the emotion (anger, joy, happiness, fear). Then write down what pops into your mind that initiated feelings of "not being good enough" or "worthy."

After identifying the energy that holds you back, you may release the negative beliefs by using The Sedona Method® of Release. Use the Journal Page to write about the negative belief or thought pattern and your experience in releasing them.

SQUARE OF LIFE — IDENTIFYING FEELINGS/ENERGY SOURCE

HEALTH	**WEALTH**
Descriptive word: _____ Feelings of not being good enough or worthy stem from:	Descriptive word: _____ Feelings of not being good enough or worthy stem from:
LOVE	**PERFECT SELF-EXPRESSION**
Descriptive word: _____ Feelings of not being good enough or worthy stem from:	Descriptive word: _____ Feelings of not being good enough or worthy stem from:

THE CONSCIOUS MIND

The conscious mind is aware of the physical world. It is our outer voice of continual mind chatter — active thoughts and words. This part of us sees and takes in all that goes on around us. What we take into our minds is fed to our subconscious, such as negative news, negative movies, negative music, worry, gossip, fear, and hatred — all negative things. Positive things that we take in are also initiated into the subconscious, such as love, joy, and happiness.

Remember, everything we do, say, or think is either love or fear based. There is no in between.

4 ▶ INSIDE ASSIGNMENT

Mental Diet What does your conscious/subconscious diet consist of?

Everything we do, say, or think is either love or fear based. There is no in between. In order to attract the relationships, health, finances, and work that you desire, you must shift from a fear source diet to a LOVE SOURCE diet. Use the Journal Page to explore in depth what you discovered about yourself.

If you live your life on a diet of negativity, you are living your life from fear source and drawing to you all that exists at the lower vibration of fear — things you do not want. Step back as an observer and discern how many of the following from the list apply to you.

LOVE SOURCE

Smiling

Laughing

Experiencing Joy

Experiencing Happiness

Feeling Harmonious

Feeling Balanced

Complimenting Others

Loving Others

Blessing Others

Praying for Others

Praying for Yourself

Loving Yourself

FEAR SOURCE

Gossip

Resentment

Complaining

Criticism of Others

Sarcasm

Unforgiveness

Criticism of Yourself

Anger

Judgment of Yourself

Judgment of Others

Hostility

Worry

Hatred

Frustration

Anxiety

Stress

Fear

Anything Less than Love

Negativity of Any Kind…

INNER AND OUTER VOICES

As the observer you see firsthand the thought patterns that make up your daily behavior. The more quickly you identify the negative lower vibrating fear-based thought patterns, the more quickly you can use your tools to transform them to positive thought patterns of the higher vibration of love.

It is the inner voice of the subconscious and the outer voice of the conscious that must be in alignment to elevate our energetic vibration to match that of what we desire to manifest into our lives.

5 ▶ INSIDE ASSIGNMENT

Reaping What You Sow   The purpose of this exercise is to discern if your inner and outer voices are in unison with regard to what you wish to create in your life. Write down a desire you would like to experience in your life on the first line. How does creating what you want feel within your body? Does it resonate, or do you feel resistance? Where do you feel the resistance in your body? Why do you feel it? Does your ego whisper or scream to you, "you can't have that," or "you can't do that"?

Write down the first three things that pop into your head concerning how you feel about the possibility of creating what you want. Don't give it a lot of thought, just write it down. If you overthink the exercise, your subconscious may talk you out of acknowledging what you believe about your abilities to have what you want.

If you feel any resistance at all, then your inner voice of the subconscious and the outer voice of your conscious are not in alignment.

I want _____

1. _____

2. _____

3. _____

THE SHIFT FROM FEAR TO LOVE

Before now, in all probability, negative thoughts were rampant in your brain. The key is to identify negativity and transmute that negative fear-based thought to one that is loving and positive. Excellent tools to help you maintain the higher vibration of positive love is the book *The Ten Be's of Positivity* by positivoligist Lynette Turner and The Game of Life Mastery Program www.GameOfLifeMastery.com.

In reality, negative, fear-based thoughts are what we think about most of the time. This is normal — it is what we are conditioned to do. This next exercise is designed to anchor positive, love-based thoughts as your normal daily thought pattern — to live from a point of love — eliminating fear and negativity from your life.

The goal is to make it through the day thinking or saying the least amount of negative things. Set the intent now to eliminate negativity from your life. Begin today by identifying negative thoughts and things you say.

▶6 INSIDE ASSIGNMENT

Living from Love or Fear For the next seven days, beginning today, fill out the My Life — Love Source or Fear Source Form. Under Living from Love Source write down the positive things you participated in each day, such as smiling at someone, helping someone, reading positive information, complimenting someone sincerely, blessing someone or something, praying, etc. Under Living from Fear Source write down the negative things you participated in each day, such as taking in negative news, gossiping, snapping at or arguing with someone, feeling hatred or anger within toward someone or something. At the end of each day, review the negative and positive experiences.

You cannot fail at this. Negative thoughts are going to come into your mind — you live in a physical world laced with negativity. Do NOT beat yourself up for negative thoughts — this only adds to the negativity. Instead be elated and proud of yourself that you noticed negative thoughts.

Do you find your life consisting of negativity more than positivity? Are you seeing the negative made manifest in your life from your thoughts? What can you do to become more positive? Do you see how the negative things are based in fear? Do you see how the positive are based in love?

With diligence you will have fewer and fewer negative thoughts. You may find that you don't have much to say in the beginning, because you're eliminating negative speech as well.

If your positive side is longer than your negative, you're ahead of the game — congratulations!

Continue actively monitoring your thoughts from this day forward to heal fear-based negative thought patterns and beliefs and replace them with love-based positive thought patterns and beliefs to step into and stay in your power! Remember all thoughts are either fear based or love based.

The more you fill your life with love-based thoughts, the more love-based people, situations, events, and material things the Universe will "match" to you. This is how the Universe works with you, with everyone, everywhere, all the time. This is the Law of Attraction.

Remember, even though the physical world conditioning has taught you that fear and negativity is the way life is and they are forever to be the basis of your life, it isn't true. You have the choice to select whether your continual line of thinking and believing is based in fear and lack or love and prosperity. *You have the choice.* You will see and experience more prosperity in your life as you eliminate negativity and live from a love-based foundation!

Use the Personal Journal to write about your experiences.

LIVING FROM LOVE OR FEAR

Living from Love Source   **Living from Fear Source**

Day 1 _____   _____

Day 2 _____   _____

Day 3 _____   _____

Day 4 _____   _____

Day 5 _____   _____

Day 6 _____   _____

Day 7 _____   _____

THE SUPERCONSCIOUS MIND

The superconscious is our Higher Self or Divinity within. It is here we find the guidance of our intuition. It is here that our Field of Potentiality — all that we dream — resides. It is already ours! It is up to us as to either allow it into our reality by shifting into the love source, or continue to block it with the lower energy of fear.

The Higher Self within is the essence of who we are — spiritual beings experiencing a human existence. Once you tap that inner knowing and guidance your heart will be open to working with your Higher Self in the space of unconditional love. Deepak Chopra teaches in his book, *The Seven Spiritual Laws of Success*, of meeting our Authentic (higher) Self in the silence of not speaking. It is in the silence of meeting with our Authentic Self that our heart expands into the space of pure potentiality, the space of all creation where we live from a foundation of love without fear.

The following exercise is designed to help you connect with the essence of who you are and "remember" what it feels like. For those of you who meditate, you already know how to connect with the Divinity within you. For those of you who are new to meditation, you may download a free, easy-to-use step-by-step guided meditation, "Tap into Your Higher Self" by going to: www.GameOfLifeMastery.com/freegift. This bonus tool will open the door to connecting with not only your Higher Self but with those of the angelic realm as well. The next Inside Assignment takes you through this process.

▶ 7   INSIDE ASSIGNMENT

Looking Within Through Meditation to Meet Your Higher Self, read the entire exercise before you begin. Meditation can be used to quiet the mind to connect with the essence of who you are: your Higher Self. If you have trouble quieting your mind to experience the meditative state, you may download a free, easy-to-use step-by-step guided meditation "Tap into Your Higher Self" recorded specifically for *The Game of Life Workbook* by going to www.GameOfLifeMastery.com/freegift.

Set your connection intention: sit quietly and breathe deeply. In prayer, surround yourself with God's Divine White Light of protection and ask that only those of the light be allowed to communicate with you. Ask your angels and guides to help you to look within and connect with your Higher Self.

When you make this connection, look deeply at what you believe about yourself to identify thought patterns and beliefs that may no longer serve you. You may ask your Higher Self questions and for guidance.

When you finish, return to the physical world and thank those of the angelic realm for their help in making your connection.

The more you practice the intent to connect with your Higher Self, the more you will understand the Divine guidance within you to create the highest possible outcome in your relationships and life situations. Use the Journal Page to write about what you have discovered.

TAPPING INTO THE QUIET VOICE WITHIN

Recognizing and truly listening to the quiet voice within us takes practice and patience and is completely possible. Once we identify the part of our body that gives us the "yes" or "no" answer all we have to do is allow ourselves to relax and experience the sharing of God.

 INSIDE ASSIGNMENT

Connecting Within Take a deep breath and read the following statements. Discern where you feel a response in your body. Identify where you feel a true sensation of clarity — whether it's in your solar plexus, heart center, or another area of your body.

"Healthy grass grows green in color."

Do you feel clarity in your solar plexus___   heart___ other_____

Where you felt the clarity is your "Truth Center." This is what a "Yes" answer feels like.

Now identify the feeling created by this statement: "Healthy grass grows orange in color."

This feeling should be an angst or disagreeing feeling in the same area — your truth center. Notice the difference in the feeling? This is what a "No" answer feels like.

Now we know what a "Yes" answer feels like and what a "No" answer feels like. Work with this exercise to tune in with this energy of "yes" and "no."

The more you set this intent and practice it, the easier it will be to understand the "yes" and "no" answers of your highest good. You may use this exercise of tapping into your Intuition/Truth Center as a staple in making decisions. Begin with easy questions; once you get the hang of it, then you may use it with confidence on the bigger questions. Use the Journal Page to write about what you have discovered about your quiet voice within.

To learn more about your Intuition/Truth Center/Higher Self within, you may refer to the book *A Still, Small Voice* by Echo Bodine and the Game of Life Mastery Program found at www.GameOfLifeMastery.com.

THE ENEMY IS WITHIN — FEAR

Florence states that man's only enemy is fear — fear of lack, fear of failure, fear of sickness, fear of loss. Fear is a physical world conditioning. As babies we do not come into this world with fear in our hearts; it is a learned response and becomes a normal part of our lives, like breathing. Fear keeps us from experiencing joy, love, peace, and happiness.

Conversations with God, by Neale Donald Walsch, tells us that man created his greatest enemy through doubt — "FEAR."

Fear is the pain of an event that has not happened yet.

Jesus Christ said: "Why are ye fearful, oh ye of little faith?"

Everything we do, everything we say, everything we think, is either based in love or in fear. It is the enlightened who know that there is a choice — to fear, or not to fear. Some think they don't live in fear source, but the fact is most simply don't recognize it as such.

Fear is a self-made illusion and does not exist in the super-conscious where our highest potential resides. As stated previously, fear is a learned response. When we experience something our human brain naturally reacts by pulling forth and comparing a past event to the current event to predict the future.

Think about the dreams that have eluded you.

What has stopped you from pursuing these dreams? Is fear a huge factor? What about limiting beliefs and thought patterns that are based in fear? Perhaps the negativity of others holds you back — what would they think?

Good things in your life are not rewards for good behavior. You are a profoundly loved child of God and it is your birthright to receive good things.

Once you realize how FEAR has held you captive, you'll see you have a choice. You've identified that fear is a factor in your life. Do you choose to live in fear or do you choose to live in love?

Fear is tricky because we've lived with it for so long; it is a part of us. Fear disguises itself, hiding in our subconscious until we make the effort to identify it and heal it.

▶ 9 ▶ INSIDE ASSIGNMENT

Finding the Fear Sit quietly and think about the dreams you have had for the following items. Under each item write about your dreams as they relate to each topic.

Identify in your body where you feel the fear that held you back from fulfilling your dreams. Refer to The Sedona Method® of Release or the free bonus, Shift Your Energy to Love found at www.GameOfLifeMastery.com/freegift. Use the procedure that works for you until you no longer feel the fear sensations within that have prevented you from fulfilling your dreams.

Use the Journal Page to write about your experience in releasing the fear-based feelings. You will begin to see changes as a result of the experience of releasing. You are shifting from within and the fear has no choice but to shift as well!

SOUL PURPOSE AND THE NEW PARADIGM

Our Soul Purpose is to reconnect with the essence of which we are, love, and bring all aspects of ourselves into alignment as love source. The secret to shifting into love source is to HEAL within all the pain of not only this lifetime but past lifetimes as well.

Consciously we must work to heal from deep within core issues and beliefs that harbor fear. Often times when we heal an issue within, fear in other areas of our life will also dissipate or be revealed.

You may have already experienced dissolving a fear issue and then learned there is yet more of it months later. *This happens because we are as an onion and we can only release fear at the level of our understanding.* As we grow and evolve, elevating our vibration higher and higher in love source, yet more fear is revealed to us to release and resolve. Finding more fear is exciting because it is a sign that we've elevated our vibrational frequency higher. When we vibrate at a higher level we easily create new, exciting, wonderful things, life events and relationships, as our reality. Vibrating at a higher level also strengthens our light to illuminate yet more suppressed fear. When we work through this newly revealed fear, we are then able to move to yet a higher vibration of love.

The energies affecting the planet are revealing long suppressed fears. When we shift to the higher vibration of love, new opportunities of limitless possibility are revealed.

DIVINE LIFE PATH

We are conditioned by the teachings of the physical world to live in fear. The act of living in fear makes us a magnet for unhappy, unhealthy situations, events, and relationships. As we live our lives in the physical world of earth, our spiritual self may become buried beneath the conditioning of fear-based

IDENTIFYING HIDDEN FEARS

My Dream	How It Will Affect Me	How It Will Affect Others	Reason for Hesitation	Hidden Fear
Personal Adventures				
Help Others in Need				
Self-Worth/Personal Growth				
Relationship Needs or Changes				

thoughts and beliefs. The more buried we become, the more lost and scattered we are, unsure of not only where we are going, our goals and our beliefs, but who we truly are.

Florence states that "many people are in ignorance of their true destinies and are striving for things and situations which do not belong to them, and would only bring failure and dissatisfaction if attained."

Each one of us has our own Field of Potentiality that consists of our Perfect Square of Life. Often times we see something (material or otherwise) that someone else has and we want it just because they have it — not because it is something we truly desire. This material item, relationships, etc., are in their Field of Potentiality — not ours. We are magnificent manifestors, therefore, when we focus our thoughts on attaining what they have, we manifest it into our lives and it brings failure and dissatisfaction to us.

As we live in the physical world, most of us float through our lives, floundering around, trying to get a grip on goals, dreams, reality, fear, happiness, and we live "unconsciously." We ask ourselves, "Just what are we really supposed to be doing?"

We're scattered because we're not connecting with our Higher Self.

Each one of us has a Divine Life Path, the path of spiritual enlightenment — of spiritual growth — the path of healing to unconditional love. That is what we are all here to do, to heal from deep within and vibrate at a level of consciousness that accepts and allows unconditional love. We are here to create Heaven on Earth.

How do we find our true Divine Life Path and create our version of Heaven on Earth?

We look within. We connect with the Life Force Energy of Creation within and shift into that vibration of love energy.

THE DIVINE SELECTION/DIVINE RIGHT

Asking God to send to us the Divine Selection is allowing the Law of Substitution to bring to us our highest good. We are asking to receive what we desire or its equivalent.

To receive what is "best" for us we must learn to "ask aright." We must connect with God and imprint in our superconscious the trust in allowing God to provide for us what is best, what we desire or its equivalent. Everything we desire falls into one of the four categories of the Square of Life: Health, Wealth, Love, and Perfect Self-Expression. God has prosperous abundance for each of us in all these areas. Can we trust Him to provide it — to be our supply?

Example: The woman who was, in reality, in love with the wrong man. Florence asked God/The Universe for the right man — the "divine selection" — the man who belonged to her by Divine Right. In so doing, free will was used wisely to ask for that which was her highest good, hers by "Divine Right."

By trusting and having faith in the Divine Selection, the woman opened the doors to receive what was hers by "Divine Right," her highest good. Even though originally she wanted another man, she practiced free will, trust, and faith and received abundance in love: the "Divine Selection by Divine Right."

FIELD OF POTENTIALITY, BIRTHRIGHT, MANIFESTING ABUNDANCE

Jesus Christ said the Kingdom is within us. The Kingdom is our Field of Potentiality.

Each one of us has a Field of Potentiality or Kingdom, where all our dreams and desires reside. Every wish, every desire is a demand and is created the instant we formulate the desire in our minds — it is IN our Field of Potentiality vibrating at a specific vibration, a vibration without fear. All we need to do to manifest it into our reality is to elevate our energetic vibration to match it. It is our own limiting beliefs that block us from receiving all that make up our dreams and desires.

Florence states that the imagination is the "scissors of the mind," ever creating the reality of our lives. The imagination or "imaging faculty" is based on the energy of thoughts and beliefs in our subconscious and externalizes or mirrors into our lives.

Healing or shifting from within to change our lives is the new paradigm of living. We've learned that we are energy and all that we desire is energy. So now we're seeing the bigger picture, that all we need to do to create something different is to shift the energy from the old that no longer serves us to the new.

Our thoughts and our words are energy — that which we ask for, that which we continually think of will manifest into our lives. It is up to us as to whether it is our highest good or idle words and thoughts leading to disaster.

Trust and faith in God/the Universe as our supply in all things will bring us the prosperous abundance in all things that we desire. In looking within and finding that inner light of God within us, we find it easier to trust and practice active faith in God's abilities.

To achieve this level of consciousness, our subconscious must be in order.

REWRITING THE SUBCONSCIOUS RECORDS

Florence tells us that "every thought, every word is impressed" upon our subconscious and carried out in amazing detail, just like a record or computer memory chip. This is the Law of Attraction. Unfortunately the details in our subconscious have been unconsciously written (or programmed) through negative conditioning of the physical world — fear, lack, anger, frustration, jealously, resentment, etc. Our goal is to delete from our subconscious these records of negativity and rewrite them with love, grace, and the complete faith and trust in the knowledge of the limitless possibilities that we are.

The stages to Rewriting the Subconscious are:
1. Identifying the fear, especially the fears we hide from ourselves.

2. Releasing the fear we identified.

3. Connecting with the Higher Self within us.

4. Shifting fear source energy into love source energy — rewriting our subconscious records.

INFINITE INTELLIGENCE — GOD IS EVER READY!

Florence states that "Infinite Intelligence, God, is ever ready to carry out man's smallest or greatest demands." It is our birthright — not selfishness or greed.

We do not come here to the physical world alone. At any given moment of any given day we are a crowd of angels, guides, and teachers, as well as deceased loved ones. We come here with this entourage to help us achieve the spiritual growth and reconnect to God's love source by healing fear within us.

Some religions teach us that we cannot talk to God directly. This simply is NOT true. We can communicate directly with God to ask for help or just to chat. God, the angels, as well as our guides and teachers, are with us in every moment to help us grow and heal as we travel our divine life path. They diligently work behind the scenes to help us without interfering in our free will. In order to receive more of their help, all we have to do is implement our free will and ask.

RECAP

The first chapter, The Game, opens our eyes to the realization that our words, actions, and even our thoughts are very real, very powerful energy. We've discovered that there are deep-seated beliefs — many we aren't even aware of having — some possibly coming from a past life, that create our reality.

We've learned of the workings of the three levels of consciousness and the tools to work as one with God instead of floundering aimlessly on our own. In explaining the levels of consciousness, Florence gives us insight into connecting to the Higher Self.

Allow yourself the time it takes to absorb and digest all the information. You're shifting and healing the fear source within you and creating a magnificent foundation of love in which to begin the creation of the life of your dreams. This shift has begun a ripple affect of love that will wave out into your physical life. As within, it is without.

That which cannot deal with this wave of love source will leave your Square of Life — it could be difficult relationships, health issues, anything. Know that when something leaves your life, a void is created and the Universe rushes to fill it. Now that you are vibrating at the higher vibration of love, the Universe will match to you people and life situations that are vibrating at this higher love vibration from your Field of Potentiality.

The Game of Life is filled with repetition. This is how we learn. Each time we return to a subject throughout the book, we will have acquired a higher level of consciousness. Each time the workbook is opened we are at a new level of understanding, and a new level of consciousness is introduced and experienced.

May you be profoundly blessed in this moment and every moment after.

PERSONAL JOURNAL

PERSONAL JOURNAL

CHAPTER 2

The Law of Prosperity

■ ■ ■ ■ ■

One of the greatest messages given to the race through the scriptures is that God is man's supply and that man can release, *through his spoken word,* all that belongs to him by Divine Right. He must, however, have *perfect faith in his spoken word.*

Isaiah said, "My word shall not return unto me void, but shall accomplish that where it is sent." We know now, that words and thoughts are tremendous vibratory forces, ever molding man's body and affairs.

A woman came to me in great distress and said she was to be sued on the fifteenth of the month for three thousand dollars. She knew no way of getting the money and was in despair.

I told her God was her supply, and *that there is a supply for every demand.*

So I spoke the word! I gave thanks that the woman would receive three thousand dollars at the right time in the right way. I told her she must have perfect faith, and act her *perfect faith.* The fifteenth came but no money had materialized.

She called me on the phone and asked what she was to do.

I replied, "It is Saturday, so they won't sue you today. Your part is to act rich, thereby showing perfect faith that you will receive it by Monday." She asked me to lunch with her to keep up her courage. When I joined her at a restaurant, I said, "This is no time to economize. Order an expensive luncheon, act as if you have already received the three thousand dollars."

"All things whatsoever ye ask in prayer, *believing,* ye shall receive." "You must act as if you *had already received.*" The next morning she called me on the phone and asked me to stay with her during the day. I said, "No, you are divinely protected and God is never too late."

In the evening she phoned again, greatly excited and said, "My dear, a miracle has happened! I was sitting in my room this morning, when the doorbell rang. I said to the maid, 'Don't let anyone in.' The maid, however, looked out the window and said, 'It's your cousin with the long white beard.'

"So I said, 'Call him back. I would like to see him.' He was just turning the corner, when he heard the maid's voice, and *he came back*.

"He talked for about an hour, and just as he was leaving he said, 'Oh, by the way, how are finances?'

"I told him I needed the money, and he said, 'Why, my dear, I will give you three thousand dollars the first of the month.'

"I didn't like to tell him I was going to be sued. What shall I do? I won't *receive it till* the first of the month, and I must have it tomorrow. I said, 'I'll keep on treating.'"

I said, "Spirit is never too late. I give thanks she has received the money on the invisible plane and that it manifests on time." The next morning her cousin called her up and said, "Come to my office this morning and I will give you the money." That afternoon, she had three thousand dollars to her credit in the bank, and wrote checks as rapidly as her excitement would permit her.

If one asks for success and prepares for failure, he will get the situation he has prepared for. For example: A man came to me asking me to speak the word that a certain debt would be wiped out.

I found he spent his time planning what he would say to the man when he did not pay his bill, thereby neutralizing my words. He should have seen himself paying the debt.

We have a wonderful illustration of this in the Bible, relating to the three kings who were in the desert, without water for their men and horses. They consulted the prophet Elisha, who gave them this astonishing message:

"Thus saith the Lord — Ye shall not see wind, neither shall ye see rain, yet make this valley full of ditches."

Man must prepare for the thing he has asked for, *when there isn't the slightest sign of it in sight.*

For example: A woman found it necessary to look for an apartment during the year when there was a great shortage of apartments in New York. It was considered almost an impossibility, and her friends were sorry for her and said, "Isn't it too bad, you'll have to store your furniture and live in a hotel." She replied, *"You needn't feel sorry for me, I'm a superman, and I'll get an apartment."*

She spoke the words: *"Infinite Spirit, open the way for the right apartment."* She knew there was a supply for every demand, and that she was "unconditioned," working on the spiritual plane, and that "one with God is a majority."

She had contemplated buying new blankets, when *the "tempter,"* the adverse thought or reasoning mind, suggested, "Don't buy the blankets, perhaps, after all, you won't get an apartment and you will have no use for them." She promptly replied (to herself): "I'll dig my ditches by buying the blankets!" So she prepared for the apartment — acted as though she already had it.

She found one in a miraculous way, and it was given to her although there were over *two hundred other applicants.*

The blankets showed active faith.

It is needless to say that the ditches dug by the three kings in the desert were filled to overflowing. (Read, II Kings)

Getting into the spiritual swing of things is no easy matter for the average person. The adverse thoughts of doubt and fear surge from the subconscious. They are the "army of the aliens" that must be put to flight. This explains why it is so often, "darkest before the dawn."

A big demonstration is usually preceded by tormenting thoughts.

Having made a statement of high spiritual truth, one challenges the old beliefs in the subconscious, and "error is exposed" to be put out.

This is the time when one must make his affirmations of truth repeatedly, and rejoice and give thanks that he has already received. "Before ye call I shall answer." This means that "every good and perfect gift" is already man's awaiting his recognition.

Man can only receive what he sees himself receiving.

The children of Israel were told that they could have all the land they could see. This is true of every man. He has only the land within his own mental vision. Every great work, every big accomplishment, has been brought into manifestation through holding to the vision, and often just before the big achievement, comes apparent failure and discouragement.

_____

_____

_____

_____

_____

_____

_____

_____

_____

_____

_____

_____

_____

_____

_____

The children of Israel, when they reached the "Promised Land," were afraid to go in, for they said it was filled with giants who made them feel like grasshoppers. "And there we saw the giants and we were in our own sight as grass-hoppers." This is almost every man's experience.

However, the one who knows spiritual law is undisturbed by appearance, and rejoices while he is "yet in captivity." That is, he holds to his vision and gives thanks that the end is accomplished, he has received.

Jesus Christ gave a wonderful example of this. He said to his disciples: "Say not ye, there are yet four months and then cometh the harvest? Behold, I say unto you, lift up your eyes and look on the fields; for they are ripe already to harvest." His clear vision pierced the "world of matter" and he saw clearly the fourth dimensional world, things as they really are, perfect and complete in Divine Mind. So man must ever hold the vision of his journey's end and demand the manifestation of that which he has already received. It may be his perfect, health, love, supply, self-expression, home, or friends.

They are all finished and perfect ideas registered in Divine Mind (man's own superconscious mind) and must come through him, not to him. For example: A man came to me asking for treatments for success. It was imperative that he raise, within a certain time, fifty thousand dollars for his business. The time limit was almost up when he came to me in despair. No one wanted to invest in his enterprise, and the bank had flatly refused a loan. I replied: "I suppose you lost your temper while at the bank, therefore your power. You can control any situation if you first control yourself." "Go back to the bank," I added, "and I will treat." My treatment was: "You are identified in love with the spirit of everyone connected with the bank. Let the divine idea come out of this situation." He replied, "Woman, you are talking about an impossibility. Tomorrow is Saturday; the bank closes at twelve, and my train won't get me there until ten, and the time limit is up tomorrow, and anyway they won't do it. It's too late." I replied, "God doesn't need any time and is never too late. With Him all things are possible." I added, "I don't know anything about business, but I know all about God." He replied: "It all sounds fine when I sit here listening to you, but when I go out it's terrible." He lived in a distant city, and I did not hear from him for a week, then came a letter. It read: "You were right. I raised the money, and will never again doubt the truth of all that you told me."

I saw him a few weeks later, and I said, "What happened? You evidently had plenty of time, after all." He replied, "My train was late, and I got there just fifteen minutes to twelve. I walked into the bank quietly and said, 'I have come for the loan,' and they gave it to me without a question."

It was the last fifteen minutes of the time allotted to him, and Infinite Spirit was not too late. In this instance the man could never have demonstrated alone. He needed someone to help him hold to the vision. This is what one man can do for another.

Jesus Christ knew the truth of this when he said: "If two of you shall agree on earth as touching anything that they shall ask, it shall be done for them of my Father which is in heaven." One gets too close to his own affairs and becomes doubtful and fearful.

The friend or "healer" sees clearly the success, health, or prosperity, and never wavers, because he is not close to the situation.

It is much easier to "demonstrate" for someone else than for one's self, so a person should not hesitate to ask for help, if he feels himself wavering.

A keen observer of life once said, "No man can fail, if some one person sees him successful." Such is the power of the vision, and many a great man owes his success to a wife, or sister, or a friend who "believed in him" and held without wavering to the perfect pattern!

WORKBOOK SESSION TWO

The Law of Prosperity

Topics:

- God Is My Supply!

- Money Is Energy

- In the Moment and Calm Assertive Energy

- Prepare for Receipt!

- The Gratitude of Receipt

- Manifestation Comes Through Us — Not to Us

- Recap and Personal Journal

Begin this session by breathing deeply to achieve balance. Surround yourself with God's Divine White Light of Protection and set your intention to connect with your Higher Self.

Father, Mother, God, Creator of All That Is…

I claim my personal power and open the way to see clearly my Field of Potentiality, my field of infinite possibilities. I cut the ties of beliefs and thought patterns that no longer serve me in all directions of time, removing them from my consciousness, my subconscious, and my superconscious. I fearlessly step into the magnificence of the true essence of who I am — One with God. I graciously accept all that is mine by Divine Right, under grace in a miraculous way and commit to fulfill all that I came to be, have, and do in this incarnation on Mother Earth at this time.

Amen

Ask your guides, angels, and teachers to be present with you to help you open your heart, mind, and spirit to the infinite possibilities of you.

God Is My Supply!

In Chapter 1, we explored your thought patterns, beliefs and focus that have created your life to date. We are in agreement that you are the one in the driver's seat and you are definitely the one who is doing the breathing. YOU are in charge! You now understand that in order to create the change you desire in your life, you must take full responsibility for creating the life that you are living.

Florence states that "One of the greatest messages given to the race through the scriptures is that God is man's supply and that man can release, through his spoken word, all that belongs to him by Divine Right. He must, however, have perfect faith in his spoken word."

In Chapter 2, The Law of Prosperity, Florence opens the way for us to fully understand how tremendously powerful we truly are. This translates to the fact that our lives aren't created by an unseen hand dishing out happy and unhappy experiences. We are each powerful creators and WE create all our experiences, both happy and unhappy.

In the previous workbook session we talked about how good things that manifest into our lives are not rewards for good behavior. Each one of us is a profoundly loved child of God — we are One with God. To get our minds around this we must release a lot of physical world conditioning and teaching and also accept that God is a loving God — not judgmental and punishing.

Father, Mother, God is of love source. In reconnecting with the essence of who we are, love, we reconnect as One with God and open the way to receive all that is in our "Kingdom," or Field of Potentiality.

Now that we understand that WE are the creators of our lives, not circumstances, then we have the power to create something different. Florence teaches: "Man releases, through your spoken word, all that belongs to you by Divine Right."

This reiterates that all we dream of is in our Field of Potentiality AND that we have dominion as Master Creators to draw our dreams into our reality. We do so by matching our energy to the energy of what we desire — not by matching our bank account to it.

MONEY IS ENERGY

The physical world teaches that money will solve our problems and that in order to fulfill our dreams and desires, we must have an abundance of money. If you take in the subliminal teachings of commercials we need money to have love and good health, too.

Money will NOT solve your problems. How do you feel about this statement?

The reality is that we don't need a pile of money to manifest what we desire. Money is simply energy, just like everything else. If money is required, the Universe will provide the way for the money to manifest to fulfill our desire. This is true because we live in an abundant Universe with an infinite supply of everything — including money!

Never ASK for money in order to manifest something you want, because asking for money limits the ways the Universe can provide, or match to you your desires.

INSIDE ASSIGNMENT

Money and Problems Ponder this statement. Money will NOT solve my problems. Do you understand the validity of this statement, or do you believe money will solve all or perhaps some of your problems? Be honest and write down how you feel below.

_____

_____

_____

_____

_____

_____

_____

In reviewing the feelings you've written down you will clearly see where some of your most deeply seated fears exist. Use the Sedona Method® of Release or Bonus Gift: "Shift Your Energy to Love" technique to shift this fear energy to love energy to dissipate your fear. You may download the bonus gift at www.GameOfLifeMastery.com/freegift.

Use the Personal Journal to explore your feelings.

IN THE MOMENT AND CALM ASSERTIVE ENERGY

Florence shares with us the example of the woman who needed three thousand dollars right away. Florence spoke the word and gave thanks that the woman would receive the money at the right time in the right way. Florence helped the woman to shift her energy concerning the money by counseling her to have perfect faith and to act the perfect faith. Together they shifted the energy of money to be the same as everything else — as attainable as breathing in fresh air.

All three departments of the mind were employed.

1. The **Conscious** mind activated the delivery of the money by "speaking the word," claiming the money without fear, as if claiming more air to breathe. By claiming the money without fear, she shifted her energy to the higher state of love.

   Florence's energy was unwavering in her conviction that the money was in her client's Field of Potentiality. Her energy behind the "Treatment" was of "Calm Assertive Energy," matter of fact, without question, doubt, or fear. Florence was "in the moment" without influences of the past or the "what ifs" of the future. Her "Treatments of Speaking the Word" were powerful because she knew the client's desires were in her "Kingdom," or Field of Potentiality, because we live in an abundant Universe, an unlimited supply warehouse, with more than enough for everyone — whether the client knew it or not.

2. The **Subconscious** mind recorded the energy of receiving the money through repetition of giving thanks for having received. Stepping fully into the energy of gratitude of receipt anchored her shift from fear source to love.

3. The **Superconscious** then recognized the shift in energy from the lower vibration of fear to the higher vibration of love and worked with the Universe to "match" to the woman that which she desired from her "Kingdom," or Field of Potentiality.

By aligning her inner and outer voices in all three departments of the mind together as a team, the woman raised her vibrational frequency of energy from fear to love and she became a magnet for the vibrational frequency of the debt paid in full and she received the money. She was based in love — no fear, no doubts, no blocks.

The way to know if your energy matches something in your Field of Potentiality is to discern if your inner and outer voices are in alignment. In the last session you learned what a "yes" and a "no" answer feels like in your Truth Center. Apply this technique to discerning if your inner and outer voices are in alignment. When they are out of alignment fear is blocking you.

PREPARE FOR RECEIPT!

Florence states that "If one asks for success and prepares for failure, he will get the situation he has prepared for." Preparing for failure splits the levels of consciousness to yet again work independently of one another, out of alignment. The vibrational level of energy stays in fear source and attracts more life situations of fear.

Preparing for success brings to full attention active faith and trust in God. Celebrating receipt of what we have asked for when there is no sign of it in sight activates true faith and trust, and aligns our vibrational frequency of energy to that of love and we become a magnet for more love!

Florence's example was of the man who asked to have a debt wiped out. Instead of moving into a state of gratitude at the debt being resolved, he instead prepared for what he was going to do when he couldn't pay the bill.

Preparing for failure manifested where his focus was: failure to receive. Preparing for failure prevents the three levels of consciousness from being in alignment and maintains the lower vibration of fear source energy.

However, we must also acknowledge that we live in a

world of duality and judgment. There is perfection in seeming failure to receive — the perfection is to allow the fear that prevented our receipt to be revealed to us so we may heal it.

A simple example of active faith is what we do when we go to a restaurant. We order our food, and have faith and trust that the cook will fulfill our order. We prepare for receipt of the meal.

When we look at active faith in this way, it sounds easy.

Florence states in Chapter 1: "Every desire, uttered or unexpressed is a demand." The instant we feel desire to receive something it is made manifest at a higher plane of existence in our Field of Potentiality. This means that all that we desire is already manifest in our "Kingdom" vibrating at the higher energetic frequency of love. When we heal fear and elevate our energetic vibration to that of love, the Universe can then match to us and manifest into our reality all that is in our Field of Potentiality.

 11 INSIDE ASSIGNMENT

Writing Your Subconscious Record This exercise is designed to help you develop your visualization skills. Think of something you want. What would it feel like to have what you want? Breathe deeply and step fully into the energy of joy you would experience at receiving what you want.

By allowing yourself to experience the feelings of already having received what you want, the emotions of receipt are activated — opulence is experienced!

Write about how you achieved the feelings of receipt and what opulence feels like in the columns.

The purpose of this exercise is to shift your energy fully to love source and achieve the feelings of Opulence, Wealth, and Affluence. Then when practicing active faith, you will know what the energy feels like in order to write the record into your subconscious for manifestation. The feelings of opulence and receipt are joyful and of love source — there is no doubt or fear.

If you feel resistance stepping into the joyful energy of receipt, look within to identify the resistance energy, then use your tools to dissipate the resistance and step fully into love energy.

Use the Journal Page to write about this experience. In the act of filling in the form and then writing about it in the journal, we anchor this process in the Subconscious — and you explore the ins and outs of the process, making it easier to implement into your life.

WRITING THE SUBCONSCIOUS RECORD

What I Desire	Visualization of Receipt	Receipt and Opulence

THE GRATITUDE OF RECEIPT

We all know what fear feels like: disappointment, anger, frustration, angst, sadness, worry, doubt, and pain. Just what does the higher vibration of gratitude and love feel like? This is a feeling within that each one of us must discern for ourselves.

When the Body World was on display at a Denver museum thousands of people viewed it. Hundreds of people went through the exhibit daily and finding a parking space was challenging and sometimes impossible. When I made reservations online to take my daughter and her friend, I also demanded the Universe to provide a parking space near the door.

We arrived at the museum in plenty of time, but could not find a parking space. Finally I dropped the girls off at the entrance. The second they shut the door I again demanded my parking place! Right in front of me someone began to back out of their space. I was shaking so hard I could barely maneuver the car into the space. For me, getting the parking place next to the front door was more exciting than the exhibit!

I remember clearly the energy I felt within me: there was no fear thinking that I might not get one — only a "Gratitude of Receipt" that a place was mine and it was up front close to the door.

MANIFESTATION COMES THROUGH US — NOT TO US

Most religions teach us that God helps those who help themselves. An interpretation of this is that God helps those when they are wise enough to ask God for help. However, the true meaning of this goes deeper to the Higher Self within. By tapping into the Higher Self within to receive what we've asked for, all receipt comes **through** us — not **to** us.

When we align the three levels of consciousness and shift into love-source energy, we become a magnet for what we desire. Therefore, our good comes through our Higher Self to manifest in our lives. It isn't just given to us, but springs forth from within us.

When you release the physical world teachings of fear you are unlimited in what you can be, do, and have. Allow yourself to step into your power as the Master Creator of your life!

 12 INSIDE ASSIGNMENT

Demand and Receipt In the previous exercise you rewrote your subconscious record. This assignment further addresses the momentum of creating what you want as your reality. Number one is an example. Write out your demand and shift the energy within you to having already received your demand.

1. I demand a parking space up front, close to the door

2. I demand _____

_____

3. I demand _____

_____

4. I demand _____

_____

5. I demand _____

_____

When you go so far as to celebrate the opulent feeling of receipt, you firmly anchor and set the record of receipt in your subconscious. As a result you powerfully create your "Demand." Practice the visualization exercise as much as you can to improve your manifesting skills and experience the high vibration of Love as opulence and gratitude. When you expand your feelings to a celebration of joy while manifesting your demand, you'll increase your energetic vibration and make yourself a powerful magnet to attract more of what you desire.

After creating your list, journal about your experiences in manifesting the items on the list.

RECAP

The second chapter, The Law of Prosperity, brings to light yet more information of how to integrate the three levels of consciousness. When integration is achieved, we create the desires of our heart as our reality.

We work in conjunction with God. We freely use our free will to live from a source of love, thereby raising our vibrational frequency to that of love to become a magnet for more love — our flow of the abundance we desire is energized!

Practice the tools of integration. Ask God questions, allow yourself to receive the answers. Practice will make working with God as easy and familiar as breathing.

Monitor your thoughts, words, and actions: are they love based or fear based? Write in your journal the happy surprises that bless your life — for now you are consciously opening the door to receive that which you desire!

God is lighting your Divine Life Path with the glow of spiritual love and wisdom.

May you be profoundly blessed in this moment and in every moment after.

PERSONAL JOURNAL

_____

_____

_____

_____

_____

_____

_____

_____

_____

_____

PERSONAL JOURNAL

_____

_____

_____

_____

_____

_____

_____

_____

_____

_____

_____

_____

_____

The Power of the Word

■ ■ ■ ■ ■

A person knowing the power of the word becomes very careful of his conversation. He has only to watch the reaction of his words to know that they do "not return void." Through his spoken word, man is continually making laws for himself.

I knew a man who said, "I always miss a car. It invariably pulls out just as I arrive." His daughter said, "I always catch a car. It's sure to come just as I get there." This occurred for years. Each had made a separate law for himself, one of failure, one of success. This is the psychology of superstitions.

The horseshoe or rabbit's foot contains no power, but man's spoken word and belief that it will bring good luck creates expectancy in the subconscious mind, and attracts a "lucky situation." I find, however, this will not "work" when man has advanced spiritually and knows a higher law. One cannot turn back, and must put away "graven images." For example: Two men in my class had had great success in business for several months, when suddenly everything "went to smash." We tried to analyze the situation, and I found, instead of making their affirmations and looking to God for success and prosperity, they had each bought a "lucky monkey." I said, "Oh I see, you have been trusting in the lucky monkeys instead of God. Put away the lucky monkeys and call on the law of forgiveness," for man has power to forgive or neutralize his mistakes.

They decided to throw the lucky monkeys down a coalhole, and all went well again. This does not mean, however, that one should throw away every

_____

_____

_____

_____

_____

_____

_____

_____

_____

_____

_____

_____

_____

_____

_____

"lucky" ornament or horseshoe about the house, but he must recognize that the power behind it is the one and only power, God, and that the object simply gives him a feeling of expectancy.

I was with a friend, one day, who was in deep despair. In crossing the street, she picked up a horseshoe. Immediately, she was filled with joy and hope. She said God had sent her the horseshoe in order to keep up her courage.

It was indeed, at that moment, about the only thing that could have registered in her consciousness. Her hope became faith, and she ultimately made a wonderful demonstration. I wish to make the point clear that the men previously mentioned were depending on the monkeys, alone, while this woman recognized the power behind the horseshoe.

I know, in my own case, it took a long while to get out of a belief that a certain thing brought disappointment. If the thing happened, disappointment invariably followed. I found the only way I could make a change in the subconscious was by asserting, "There are not two powers, there is only one power, God, therefore, there are not disappointments, and this thing means a happy surprise." I noticed a change at once, and happy surprises commenced coming my way.

I have a friend who said nothing could induce her to walk under a ladder. I said, "If you are afraid, you are giving in to a belief in two powers, Good and Evil, instead of one. As God is absolute, there can be no opposing power, unless man makes the false of evil for himself. To show you believe in only one power, God, and that there is no power or reality in evil, walk under the next ladder you see."

Soon after, she went to her bank. She wished to open her box in the safe-deposit vault, and there stood a ladder in her pathway. It was impossible to reach the box without passing under the ladder. She quailed with fear and turned back. She could not face the lion on her pathway. However, when she reached the street, my words rang in her ears and she decided to return and walk under it. It was a big moment in her life, for ladders had held her in bondage for years. She retraced her steps to the vault, and the ladder was no longer there! This so often happens! If one is willing to do a thing he is afraid to do, he does not have to.

It is the law of non-resistance, which is so little understood.

Someone has said that courage contains genius and magic. Face a situation fearlessly, and there is no situation to face; it falls away of its own weight.

The explanation is that fear attracted the ladder on the woman's pathway, and fearlessness removed it.

Thus the invisible forces are ever working for man who is always "pulling the strings" himself, though he does not know it. Owing to the vibratory power of words, whatever man voices, he begins to attract. People who continually speak of disease invariably attract it.

After man knows the truth, he cannot be too careful of his words. For example: I have a friend who often says on the phone, "Do come to see me and have an old-fashioned chat." This "old-fashioned chat" means an hour of about five hundred to a thousand destructive words, the principal topics being loss, lack, failure, and sickness.

I reply: "No, I thank you. I've had enough old-fashioned chats in my life, they are too expensive, but I will be glad to have a new-fashioned chat, and talk about what we want, not what we don't want." There is an old saying that man only dares use his words for three purposes, to "heal, bless, or prosper." What man says of others will be said of him, and what he wishes for another, he is wishing for himself.

"Curses, like chickens, come home to roost."

If a man wishes someone "bad luck," he is sure to attract bad luck himself. If he wishes to aid someone to success, he is wishing and aiding himself to success.

The body may be renewed and transformed through the spoken word and clear vision, and disease be completely wiped out of the consciousness. The metaphysician knows that all disease has a mental correspondence, and in order to heal the body one must first "heal the soul."

The soul is the subconscious mind, and it must be "saved" from wrong thinking.

In the twenty-third psalm, we read: "He restoreth my soul." This means that the subconscious mind or soul must be restored with the right ideas, and the "mystical marriage" is the marriage of the soul and the spirit, or the subconscious and superconscious mind. They must be one. When the subconscious is flooded with the perfect ideas of the superconscious, God and man are one, "I and the Father are one." That is, he is one with the realm of perfect ideas; he is the man made in God's likeness and image (imagination) and is given power and dominion over all created things, his mind, body, and affairs.

_____

_____

_____

_____

_____

_____

_____

_____

_____

_____

_____

_____

_____

_____

It is safe to say that all sickness and unhappiness come from the violation of the law of love. A new commandment I give unto you, "Love one another," and in the Game of Life, love or goodwill takes every trick.

For example: A woman I know had for years an appearance of a terrible skin disease. The doctors told her it was incurable, and she was in despair. She was on the stage, and she feared she would soon have to give up her profession, and she had no other means of support. She, however, procured a good engagement and on the opening night made a great "hit." She received flattering notices from the critics, and was joyful and elated.

The next day she received a notice of dismissal. A man in the cast had been jealous of her success and had caused her to be sent away. She felt hatred and resentment taking complete possession of her, and she cried out, "Oh God don't let me hate that man." That night she worked for hours "in the silence."

She said, "I soon came into a very deep silence. I seemed to be at peace with myself, with the man, and with the whole world. I continued this for two following nights, and on the third day I found I was healed completely of the skin disease!" In asking for love, or goodwill, she had fulfilled the law ("for love is the fulfilling of the law"), and the disease (which came from subconscious resentment) was wiped out.

Continual criticism produces rheumatism, as critical, inharmonious thoughts cause unnatural deposits in the blood, which settle in the joints.

False growths are caused by jealousy, hatred unforgiveness, fear, etc. Every disease is caused by a mind not at ease. I said once, in my class, "There is no use asking anyone 'What's the matter with you?' we might just as well say, 'Who's the matter with you?'" Unforgiveness is the most prolific cause of disease. It will harden arteries or liver and affect eyesight. In its train are endless ills.

I called on a woman, one day, who said she was ill from having eaten a poisoned oyster. I replied, "Oh, no, the oyster was harmless, you poisoned the oyster. What's the matter with you?" She answered, "Oh about nineteen people." She had quarreled with nineteen people and had become so inharmonious that she attracted the wrong oyster.

Any inharmony on the external indicates there is mental inharmony. "As the within, so the without."

Man's only enemies are within himself. "And a man's foes shall be they of his own household." Personality is one of the last enemies to be overcome, as this planet is taking its initiation in love. It was Christ's message, "Peace on Earth, good will towards man." The enlightened man, therefore, endeavors to perfect himself upon his neighbor. His work is with himself, to send out goodwill and blessings to every man, and the marvelous thing is, that if one blesses a man he has no power to harm him.

For example: A man came to me asking to "treat" for success in business. He was selling machinery, and a rival appeared on the scene with what he proclaimed was a better machine, and my friend feared defeat. I said, "First of all, we must wipe out all fear, and know that God protects your interest, and that the divine idea must come out of the situation. That is, the right machine will be sold, by the right man, to the right man." And I added, "Don't hold one critical thought towards that man. Bless him all day, and be willing to not sell your machine, if it isn't the divine idea." So he went to the meeting, fearless and non-resistant, and blessing the other man. He said the outcome was very remarkable. The other man's machine refused to work, and he sold his without the slightest difficulty. "But I say unto you, love your enemies, bless them that curse you, do good to them that hate you, and pray for them that spitefully use you and persecute you."

Goodwill produces a great aura of protection about the one who sends it, and "No weapon that is formed against him shall prosper." In other words, love and goodwill destroy the enemies with one's self, therefore, one has no enemies on the external!"

There is peace on earth for him who sends goodwill to man!

WORKBOOK SESSION THREE

The Power of the Word

Topics:

- Energy: Words and Thoughts

- The Law of Non-Resistance

- Fear Is an Illusion

- Become a Miracle Magnet

- The Power of Love and Blessing

- Negativity and Physical Ailments

- Recap and Personal Journal

Begin this session by breathing deeply to achieve balance. Surround yourself with God's Divine White Light of Protection and set your intention to connect with your Higher Self.

Father, Mother, God, Creator of All That Is...

I claim my personal power and open the way to see clearly my Field of Potentiality, my field of infinite possibilities. I cut the ties of beliefs and thought patterns that no longer serve me in all directions of time, removing them from my consciousness, my subconscious, and my superconscious. I fearlessly step into the magnificence of the true essence of who I am — One with God. I graciously accept all that is mine by Divine Right, under grace in a miraculous way and commit to fulfill all that I came to be, have, and do in this incarnation on Mother Earth at this time.

Amen

Ask your guides, angels, and teachers to be present with you to help you open your heart, mind, and spirit to the infinite possibilities of you.

Man has the power to become a magnet for Abundance!

ENERGY: WORDS AND THOUGHTS

Chapter 3, The Power of the Word focuses on how our words are as seeds planting the experiences that manifest in our lives.

We're learning that words and thoughts create our reality and it is up to us as to whether they create wonderful situations in our lives or disaster. Conscious effort is required to change the conditioned thought processes that we are accustomed to.

The previous chapters and workbook sessions have referenced our deep-seated beliefs, thought patterns, and fears. Florence addresses the cause and effect of records we hold in our subconscious that affect our daily lives. She points out the affirmations we use that we don't think of as powerful, but they are.

Florence shares with us the example of the man who stated he always missed a car and his daughter who stated that she always caught a car. These are affirmations — one of negative energy and one of positive energy. Their words brought into their realities what they expected to happen. His words were negative, her words were positive and each had written and anchored into their subconscious mind an outcome.

In a workbook session of Chapter 2 you made a list of things to visualize and demand through use of your words. This exercise taught what it feels like to consistently create your desire by fearlessly using the power of your words to shift the energy and align your inner and outer voices. Using this simple, fun exercise builds confidence in using your words to create the life you desire. It also implements strong thought patterns in the form of demand as your new "Normal."

How many things do we "unconsciously" create in our realities by thoughtlessly using our words to write a negative action in our subconscious?

The next Inside Assignment helps you discern your thought processes through a variety of different situations. We also learn clearly that the Universe does NOT recognize the word "NOT." So when we say we do "not" want something, the Universe recognizes our words as a positive expression of what we desire.

For example, when you say, "I don't want to catch a cold" the Universe recognizes "I want to catch a cold." You're putting your focus on what you don't want instead of what you DO want, thereby giving it more energy and tuning INTO that energy. As a student who knows the power of the word, a better statement is: "I enjoy excellent health now and always!"

Notice the energy that is created in your mind when you say, "I don't want to catch a cold." Due to previous experiences with a cold and the less than love energy/fear associated with your words, the subconscious mind sets into motion the wheels of creating a cold.

When you say, "I enjoy excellent health now and always!" immediately, the mind takes a different course expanding the feeling of good health.

Florence states, "Man has the power to forgive or neutralize his mistakes, to have dominion over all created things, his mind, body and affairs."

This teaches us that even though we may have a negative thought pattern, belief, or statement, we can dissolve the power of it by shifting the energy and thereby changing the process we started with the negativity.

We are One with God, pulling our power from the very essence of God through us with the vibration of our words. The energetic shift we and the world are experiencing right now is forcing us to reconnect with the essence of Universal Source.

Our old way of doing things simply does NOT work any longer and we are manifesting our thoughts more quickly now than ever before. This is what we've always wanted — to manifest our desires quickly, yet many of us have not taken the time to control the power of our random thoughts and allow them to scatter about unsupervised, creating havoc and chaos. As we learn and recognize the true power of the spoken word, we are better able to create the lives we truly desire, instead of lives we really don't want.

 13 INSIDE ASSIGNMENT

The Power of Words Let's evaluate your thought patterns of unconscious creation. When you are looking for a parking place, do you think, feel, or say, "I can never find a parking place" or "I always have a parking place up front." Which is it?

Listed on the next page are a few examples of creating reality. Read each situation and the suggested "spoken word" and then write below it what you think, feel, or say on a regular basis. If your thoughts and words are negative, change them now. Make a conscious effort to use the positive viewpoint of these events and discover a magical way of living!

NOTE: The Universe does NOT recognize "not," so the message you are sending out to the Universe when you say, "I hope the bank isn't busy" is "I hope the bank **is** busy."

Use the Personal Journal Page to evaluate and write about what you have discovered about your thought processes. Are they typically negative or positive? Or did you discover that you use conjunctive words with "NOT" — e.g. "is not = isn't," "do not = doesn't." Did you learn you are continually ordering exactly what you do NOT want from the Universe?

Evaluate your thought patterns. What other affirmations do you regularly make for yourself? Are they positive or negative? Write about your findings.

MAGICAL THOUGHTS AND WORDS — THE SUBCONSCIOUS RECORDS

On the way to a place where parking can be a problem.
Suggested Spoken Word/Thought: I always get a parking place close to the door.

What I usually think: _____

Getting ready to wait in a line.
Suggested Spoken Word/Thought: I always get in the fastest-moving line.

What I usually think: _____

In anticipation of arriving at an appointed time.
Suggested Spoken Word/Thought: I always arrive at the appointed time.

What I usually think: _____

In anticipation of arriving at the bank.
Suggested Spoken Word/Thought: I always get to the bank at the "right" time.

What I usually think: _____

In anticipation of a challenging situation.
Suggested Spoken Word/Thought: I always know what to say in difficult situations.

What I usually think: _____

In anticipation of ordering food at a restaurant.
Suggested Spoken Word/Thought: The food I order will arrive promptly and taste great!

What I usually think: _____

Before a trip to the market.
Suggested Spoken Word/Thought: Every time I go shopping my needs will be met.

What I usually think: _____

THE LAW OF NON-RESISTANCE

Florence states that the Law of Non-Resistance is "little understood." When we look at it from a point of control, it is easier to understand. Beginning as babies we're taught to be in control of ourselves. It doesn't take us long to want to be in control of others as well as situations and conditions around us.

We are learning to allow our highest good to come to us through "knowing" within that what we desire is ours — this requires non-resistance. After all, we know what we want and we want it now — yes? To be in harmony with God, to be fully connected and show active faith and trust, we must allow God/the Universe to match to us what we have asked for. Patience, faith, and trust take practice.

With our thoughts and words we have the power to shift from fear energy to love energy by facing our fears. This is non-resistance. When we suppress our fears we are resistant to them. When we face our fears we are non-resistant.

The next Inside Assignment asks you to evaluate a life situation in which you are experiencing resistance. One of the examples Florence shares with us is of the man who asked her to "treat" for his business of selling his product, which was a machine. His rival claimed to have a better one, so Florence "treated" that "the right machine would be sold to the right man by the right man." She instructed her client to bless his rival and acknowledge the divine idea whether it was the sale of his product or not.

Her client followed her instructions and blessed the rival sincerely from his heart. He used his power to "heal, bless, and prosper" with his thinking and his words. He put into action the energy of wishing good for someone else, and attracted good to himself.

If we step back a moment and look at the bigger picture of this event, we see that Florence's client also experienced the "darkness before the dawn" or seeming adversity when he discovered he had a rival who sold a product like his. He then used the seeming adversity to his advantage by looking within to discern his resistance.

You may find handing an important, possibly volatile situation over to God to handle with complete trust and faith is sometimes challenging. In assessing the intricacies of such a situation, you can clearly see the workings and benefits of non-resistance.

By reaching a state of non-resistance and blessing the entire situation and all concerned with love, you will dissipate your anxiety and light the way for a pleasant outcome for everyone involved.

 INSIDE ASSIGNMENT

From Fear to Non-Resistance If we could "see" the energy our words create, we would be more careful about what we say and think.

Sit quietly and think about a situation you are experiencing that you feel is "out of your control" and causing you anxiety. Write down the situation or event in the appropriate column on the next page. Think about how you can dissipate your fear and shift your energy to a non-resistant state. What tools will you use? Prayer? Meditation? Writing/Affirmations? The Sedona Method® of Release? Bonus gift "Shift Your Energy to Love" technique (www.GameOfLifeMastery.com/freegift)?

Use the Personal Journal Page to write about the non-resistance experience from beginning to end. Evaluate if you were able to achieve complete non-resistance or if you held on to physical world conditioning and tried to control the situation. Evaluate the results. If you weren't able to reach the non-resistant state, look within again. Each time you set the intention to dissipate fear, more insight will be revealed to you. As a result you will step up in your level of understanding and the process will become easier.

SHIFTING TO NON-RESISTANCE

Situation/Event	Non-Resistance Tools	Results

FEAR IS AN ILLUSION

When we allow fear into our lives, it takes our power and controls us — as it did the woman who was afraid to walk under a ladder. When she went to the bank, a ladder was in her path so she walked away, failing to accomplish what she went there to do. Fear was in control. Then in remembering Florence's words she went back to walk under the ladder, facing her fears, and discovered the ladder was gone!

We allow this to happen to us in so many other ways. We're fearful of looking for another job when we're unhappy where we are working. We allow fear of being alone or fear of finances to keep us in unhappy relationships. We let fear control where we go and what we do, how we treat others and how we treat ourselves. Is there honor in being in a situation that makes us fearful or unhappy or depressed? We're afraid and worried about what *might* happen.

In growing up, we learn that fear is "normal" — it becomes a part of us, like breathing. Fear is a conditioning of the physical world, but it is a choice. Albeit usually an unconscious choice, it is still a choice.

Many times, over and over again, we find that the things we fear have no validity; they are but illusions. Like the woman who feared the ladder, when she faced her fears she realized her mind had deceived her into thinking her fear was a tangible object. It wasn't.

Fear is not real; it is an illusion. Remember, fear is the pain of an event that hasn't happened.

Now we have the power to choose, do we want to be fearful or do we want to live free of fear with confidence that we live in an abundant Universe and are worthy of living the life we truly desire?

This next exercise is designed to help you become aware of the many frivolous things that cause you to worry.

Worry is a sneaky form of fear, because we justify it with thoughts like, "I care, that's why I worry." As a student of Florence's, you've learned that worrying is like standing on a bridge and throwing your power over the side. There is no power in worry. However, each one of you knows that your worries and fears are very real to you. The physical world conditioning is very powerful in convincing your "reasoning mind" to take fear seriously and give it your energy.

Life happens to you whether you are worrying or not.

So what does worry do to *enhance* your life? ***Nothing.***

 INSIDE ASSIGNMENT

Why Worry? It is your job, your mission, to give to God any situations, conditions, and/or people that ignite fear or worry in your heart. This is spiritual growth into the expansion of love energy.

Sit quietly and think about what worry feels like. Look back at your day or week. Was there anything that catches your attention with the "worry" feeling? Evaluate how worry helped or made the situation worse. Did it enhance your life? Fill in the appropriate columns with your findings.

Use the Personal Journal Page to write about your experience with this exercise. What did you learn about yourself? Do you worry excessively? Did you overlook worries or fears from the previous exercises because the ones you discovered through this exercise are "normal" and you didn't recognize them as fear and/or worry? Examine your feelings. Use The Sedona Method® of Release , bonus gift "Shift Your Energy to Love" technique (www.GameOfLifeMastery.com/freegift) or The Game of Life Mastery Program (www.GameOfLifeMastery.com) to dissolve your fear/worry and heal the life event, situation, or relationship.

TO WORRY OR NOT TO WORRY

Situation or event that caused worry	Did worry change the situation or event?	Did it enhance your life to worry?

BECOME A MIRACLE MAGNET

We are "magnets" for what we continually think about. Whether we like it or believe it, this is true, this is the Law of Attraction. The Universe "matches" to us the vibrational frequency we emit. In understanding this, we now realize we have a choice. We can choose to live from fear source of negativity, doubt, and fear, attracting more of the same to us or we may choose to live from love source, maintaining an energetic Attitude of Gratitude, attracting more of the same to us.

Gratitude is amazingly powerful and will unlock the vault to access JOY in your life. Don't underestimate the power of gratitude. For many, grasping the feeling of gratitude can be elusive. There was a time in my life that I had given my power away so completely that I was drowning in chaos and fear. I was so immersed in fear that when I heard myself laugh, the sound was foreign to me. It was then that Florence's work was introduced to me and my life changed forever.

One of the concepts of Florence's teachings that I found to be miraculously powerful immediately is the passion of gratitude. Living from a basis of love with an Attitude of Gratitude will transform each of us into a Miracle Magnet!

Here is a helpful exercise designed to bring forth powerful love-based emotions at any given time, to help you reach a state of opulence in gratitude. If negative thoughts try to slip in and undermine your focus on what you truly desire, you can use the feelings of gratitude to dissipate them. This works because gratitude is of love source and there is no place for fear and/or negativity in love.

This exercise is very powerful, yet it is very easy. You can do this at any time of the day and change what you are a magnet for — negativity or miracles!

16 ▶ INSIDE ASSIGNMENT

Gratefulness Sit quietly and breathe deeply. Think about things in your life that you are grateful for. Write down at least five of them.

1. _____

2. _____

3. _____

4. _____

5. _____

As you think about them, one by one, allow yourself to experience the feelings of gratitude. Allow the feeling to grow in your body — breathe into it and embrace the feeling. Continue to breathe deeply and thank God/the Universe for all that you are grateful for.

Incorporate this exercise into your daily routine. A few minutes daily of profound gratitude will change your life! You may download the Bonus Gift: The Power of Gratitude by going to www.GameOfLifeMastery.com/freegift.

THE POWER OF LOVE AND BLESSING

Florence states, "Man's only enemies are within himself." For many of us it is easy to be resentful of someone who has something nicer than we do. But resentment strips us of our power and we hand it over with a flourish — to the one we resent. This is true of not only resentment but also anger, jealousy, and holding harsh feelings toward someone for offending us. This just doesn't sound right because "they" are the ones who did something to us, but in reality, they've moved on with their lives — we're the ones suffering from past issues. Resentment can send us on a downward spiral leading to jealousy and self-loathing and holds us hostage in "Victim Mentality."

We made the "unconscious" choice — yes, it is a choice — to give our power to someone else and allow ourselves to be crippled and vulnerable to outside influences. As a result, we become magnets for still more negativity! Without question, our subconscious and the Universal Supply Warehouse will "match" to us more negativity.

 17 INSIDE ASSIGNMENT

Love, Blessing, and Release Breathe deeply, sit quietly and think about the act of giving your power away to people following a confrontation, situation, or event.

Step outside the situation and evaluate the catalyst that prompted you to give away your power. Then look deeply within and find the feeling you experienced when you released your power. Did you find yourself immediately lost to miserable feelings? Do you experience those feelings again every time you think about the person, situation, or event?

In the Power Surrendered column on the next page, write down the event/catalyst that caused you to give away or lose control of your power. Then ask Divine Guidance to help you sincerely send love to and bless the person or situation you gave your power to. Write what you experience in the Blessing Experience column. When you bless the person or life event sincerely from your heart with love, you will feel your energy shift from less than love to love. Continue to bless this person and/or situation sincerely from the heart repeatedly until you feel the anxious resistance within you dissipate.

If you need help sending love to a life situation or relationship, use the bonus gift: "Shift Your Energy to Love" technique (www.GameOfLifeMastery.com/freegift). If you need more support, you may learn more about The Game of Life Mastery Program at www.GameOfLifeMastery.com.

BLESSING THE ENERGY SHIFT

Power Surrendered	Blessing Experience

By blessing the negativity sincerely from the heart you take your power back and transmute the situation from one of fear to one of love. In the process you become non-resistant.

This is an intensely powerful tool. It isn't an easy tool to use, because if you're upset with someone, the last thing you really want to do is bless them. That's why sincerely blessing them is so important. You must be sincere to shift your energy. Put the "sincerely from the heart" energy behind it!

Know that living in the abundance you desire is a choice, and using this tool will help you get there. Don't let the level of your emotions toward another person get between you and God. Everything is a choice. Make the best one for you.

You may use the Sedona Method or the bonus gift "Shift Your Energy to Love" technique (www.GameOfLifeMastery.com/freegift) to heal this life situation, event, or relationship. Use the Personal Journal Page to write about your experience with this exercise.

In *The Seven Spiritual Laws of Success*, Deepak Chopra teaches that "the easiest way to get what you want is to help others get what they want." So if someone has the same business, or a new house, new car, or fabulous relationship that you want, bless them to have MORE!

If Florence's client who asked her to "treat" for him to sell his machine had held ill will toward his rival, he would have planted seeds of ill will toward himself.

Being successful in blessing someone sincerely from your heart that you judge as a threat to you is profoundly healing on many levels and strongly plants the seeds of receipt of your desires.

 INSIDE ASSIGNMENT

Bless You Take just a moment and think of an individual who has something that you would like to have. It could be a wonderful relationship, a thriving business, a new car, a new house — something that you would like to have in your life. In the space below write a blessing to them to have more of what you want. Bless them sincerely from your heart without jealousy!!!

Dear _____,

I bless you sincerely from my heart to have _____

_____

_____

_____

_____

_____

Use the Personal Journal Page to explore your feelings about this exercise.

NEGATIVITY AND PHYSICAL AILMENTS

Negative thought patterns and words are toxic to the human body — TOXIC!

Florence tells us that "the body may be renewed and transformed through the spoken word and clear vision, and disease be completely wiped out of the consciousness. The metaphysician knows that all disease has a mental correspondence, and in order to heal the body one must first heal the soul. All sickness and unhappiness come from the violation of the law of love. Any inharmony on the external indicates there is mental inharmony."

If we are inharmonious on the inside due to existing in fear energy of unforgiveness, hatred, jealously, worry — anything less than love — then we draw to us on the external situations and events of the same energy.

As within, it is without.

The Law of Love tells us "Love one another." We all know what it feels like to be angry with someone, to feel jealousy and resentment. These feelings are not fun. They rob us of our joy and strip away our happiness and power. If these emotions are practiced on a daily basis, we forget to honor others and we certainly don't honor ourselves. The negativity of the emotion begins to gnaw at us and hold us captive. Our minds lose clarity and our physical bodies begin to suffer the consequences.

By understanding more of the ceaseless interaction of cause and effect, it begins to make sense that inharmony within can cause illness within the physical body.

Worry, anxiety, anger, jealousy, resentment, and hatred are mental self-poisoning emotions and thought patterns. Choosing to indulge in these feelings and thoughts maintains a state of chronic self-poisoning that destroys happiness, blocks the connection with God, leaves the body susceptible to illness and disease, and can untimely shorten the life of the physical body.

We are now able to see clearly how fear-based living will take its toll on the body. *You Can Heal Your Life* by Louise Hay is another excellent tool to help identify fear-based issues within the body.

Make the conscious choice to use the tools provided here daily. Be open to receiving the additional tools to rid yourself of suppressed fear-based thoughts and beliefs so that you may live a healthy, happy, joy-filled life of miracles!

It is your choice!

RECAP

The information contained in the Power of the Word sheds light on the day-to-day "unconscious" records we have instilled in our subconscious. Florence has given us tools to recognize and transmute the negativity to positivity.

We're opening our hearts to clearly understand just how powerful we truly are with the ability to not only change our lives but to heal our bodies and maintain good health. Chapter 3 really opens our eyes to just how powerful our words and thoughts are by itemizing the physical ailments negativity will manifest into our lives.

In traveling through your day, keep in mind the intention to integrate the three levels of consciousness. When an event or situation based in fear comes your way, use the tools you've leaned here to dissipate it. This will leave you free to continue your day in harmony. Life will be calmer, more joyful, and when you've truly mastered faith and trust in God, stress free. Can you imagine your life stress free?

It is your choice.

Journal daily if possible the changes you are experiencing within you. Also take note and journal the changes and the blessings that are filling your life.

May you be profoundly blessed in this moment and in every moment after.

PERSONAL JOURNAL

PERSONAL JOURNAL

_____

_____

_____

_____

_____

_____

_____

_____

_____

_____

_____

PERSONAL JOURNAL

_____

_____

_____

_____

_____

_____

_____

_____

_____

_____

_____

CHAPTER 4

The Law of Non-Resistance

■ ■ ■ ■ ■

Nothing on earth can resist an absolutely non-resistant person. The Chinese say that water is the most powerful element, because it is perfectly non-resistant. It can wear away a rock, and sweep all before it. Jesus Christ said, "Resist not evil," for He knew in reality, there is no evil, therefore nothing to resist. Evil has come of man's "vain imagination," or a belief in two powers, good and evil.

There is an old legend that says Adam and Eve ate of "Maya the Tree of Illusion," and saw two powers instead of one power, God.

Therefore, evil is a false law man has made for himself, through psychoma or soul sleep. Soul sleep means that man's soul has been hypnotized by the race belief (of sin, sickness, and death, etc.) that is carnal or mortal thought, and his affairs have outpictured his illusions.

We have read in a preceding chapter that man's soul is his subconscious mind, and whatever he feels deeply, good or bad, is outpictured by that faithful servant. His body and affairs show forth what he has been picturing. The sick man has pictured sickness, the poor man, poverty, the rich man, wealth.

People often ask, "why does a little child attract illness, when it is too young even to know what it means?"

I answer that children are sensitive and receptive to the thoughts of others about them, and often outpicture the fears of their parents.

I heard a metaphysician once say, "If you do not run your subconscious mind yourself, someone else will run it for you."

———————————

———————————

———————————

———————————

———————————

———————————

———————————

———————————

———————————

———————————

———————————

———————————

———————————

———————————

Mothers often, unconsciously, attract illness and disaster to their children by continually holding them in thoughts of fear, and watching for symptoms.

For example: A friend asked a woman if her little girl had had the measles. She replied promptly, "not yet!" This implied that she was expecting the illness, and therefore, preparing the way for what she did not want for herself and child.

However, the man who is centered and established in right thinking, the man who sends out only goodwill to his fellowman, and who is without fear, cannot be *touched or influenced by the negative thoughts of others.* In fact, he could then receive only good thoughts, as he himself sends forth only good thoughts.

Resistance is Hell, for it places man in a "state of torment."

A metaphysician once gave me a wonderful recipe for taking every trick in the game of life, it is the acme of non-resistance. He gave it in this way: "At one time in my life, I baptized children, and of course they had many names. Now I no longer baptize children, I baptize events, but *I give every event the same name.* If I have a failure I baptize it success, in the name of the Father, and of the Son, and of the Holy Ghost!"

In this, we see the great law of transmutation, founded on non-resistance. Through His spoken word, every failure was transmuted into success.

For example: A woman who required money, and who knew the spiritual law of opulence, was thrown continually in a business-way with a man who made her feel very poor. He talked lack and limitation and she commenced to catch his poverty thoughts, so she disliked him, and blamed him for her failure. She knew in order to demonstrate her supply, she must first feel that she *had received — a feeling of opulence must precede its manifestation.*

It dawned on her, one day, that she was resisting the situation, and seeing two powers instead of one. So she blessed the man and baptized the situation "Success!" She affirmed, "As there is only one power, God, this man is here for my good and my prosperity" (just what he did not seem to be there for). Soon after that she met, *through this man,* a woman who gave her for a service rendered, several thousand dollars, and the man moved to a distant city, and faded harmoniously from her life. Make the statement, "Every man is a golden link in the chain of my good," for all men are God in manifestation, *awaiting the opportunity given by man, himself, to serve the divine plan of his life.*

"Bless your enemy, and you rob him of his ammunition." His arrows will be transmuted into blessings.

This law is true for nations as well as individuals. Bless a nation, send love and for goodwill to every inhabitant, and it is robbed of its power to harm.

Man can only get the right idea of non-resistance through spiritual understanding. My students have often said: "I don't want to be a doormat." I reply, "when you use non-resistance with wisdom, no one will ever be able to walk over you."

Another example: One day I was impatiently awaiting for an important telephone call. I resisted every call that came in and made no outgoing calls myself, reasoning that it might interfere with the one I was awaiting.

Instead of saying, "Divine ideas never conflict, the call will come at the right time," leaving it to Infinite Intelligence to arrange, I commenced to manage things myself. I made the battle mine, not God's, and remained tense and anxious. The bell did not ring for about an hour, and I glanced at the 'phone and found the receiver had been off the hook that length of time, and the 'phone was disconnected. My anxiety, fear, and belief in interference had brought on a total eclipse of the telephone. Realizing what I had done, I commenced blessing the situation at once; I baptized it "success," and affirmed, "I cannot lose any call that belongs to me by Divine Right; I am under *grace, and not under law.*"

A friend rushed out to the nearest telephone to notify the phone company to reconnect.

She entered a crowded grocery, but the proprietor left his customers and attended to the call himself. My phone was connected at once, and two minutes later, I received a very important call, and about an hour afterward, the one I had been awaiting.

One's ships come in over a calm sea.

So long as man resists a situation, he will have it with him. If he runs away from it, it will run after him.

For example: I repeated this to a woman one day, and she replied, "How true that is! I was unhappy at home, I disliked my mother, who was critical and domineering, so I ran away and was married — but I married my mother, for my husband was exactly like my mother, and I had the same situation to face again." "Agree with thine adversary quickly."

————————————

————————————

————————————

————————————

————————————

————————————

————————————

————————————

————————————

————————————

————————————

————————————

————————————

————————————

This means, agree that the adverse situation is good, be undisturbed by it, and it falls away of its own weight. "None of these things move me," is a wonderful affirmation.

The inharmonious situation comes from some inharmony within man himself.

When there is, in him, no emotional response to an inharmonious situation, it fades away forever, from his pathway.

So we see man's work is ever with himself.

People have said to me, "Give treatments to change my husband, or my brother." I reply, "No, I will give *treatments to change you*; when you change, your husband and your brother will change."

One of my students was in the habit of lying. I told her it was a failure method and if she lied, she would be lied to. She replied, "I don't care, I can't possibly get along without lying."

One day she was speaking on the phone to a man with whom she was very much in love. She turned to me and said, "I don't trust him, I know he's lying to me." I replied, "Well, you lie yourself, so someone has to lie to you, and you will be sure it will be just the person you want the truth from." Some time after that, I saw her, and she said, "I'm cured of lying."

I questioned: "What cured you?"

She replied: "I have been living with a woman who lied worse than I did!"

One is often cured of his faults by seeing them in others.

Life is a mirror, and we find only ourselves reflected in our associates.

Living in the past is a failure method and a violation of spiritual law.

Jesus Christ said, "Behold, now is the accepted time." "Now is the day of Salvation."

Lot's wife looked back and was turned into a pillar of salt.

The robbers of time are the past and the future. Man should bless the past, and forget it if it keeps him in bondage, and bless the future, knowing it has in store for him endless joys, but live *fully in the now*.

For example: A woman came to me, complaining that she had no money with which to buy Christmas gifts. She said, "Last year was so different; I had plenty of money and gave lovely presents, and this year I have scarcely a cent."

I replied, "You will never demonstrate money while you are pathetic and live in the past. Live fully in the *now*, and *get ready to give Christmas pres-*

ents. Dig your ditches, and the money will come." She exclaimed, "I know what to do! I will buy some tinsel twine, Christmas seals, and wrapping paper." I replied, "Do that, and the *presents will come and stick themselves to the Christmas seals.*"

This too, was showing financial fearlessness and faith in God, as the reasoning mind said, "Keep every cent you have, as you are not sure you will get any more."

She bought the seals, paper, and twine, and a few days before Christmas, received a gift of several hundred dollars. Buying the seals and twine had impressed the subconscious with expectancy, and opened the way for the manifestation of the money. She purchased all the presents in plenty of time.

Man must live suspended in the moment.

"Look well, therefore, to this Day! Such is the salutation of the Dawn."

He must be spiritually alert, ever awaiting his leads, taking advantage of every opportunity.

One day, I said continually (silently), "Infinite Spirit, don't let me miss a trick," and something very important was told to me that evening. It is most necessary to begin the day with right words.

Make an affirmation immediately upon waking.

For example: *"Thy will be done this day! Today is a day of completion, I give thanks for this perfect day, miracle shall follow miracle and wonders shall never cease."*

Make this a habit, and one will see wonders and miracles come into his life.

One morning I picked up a book and read, "Look with wonder at that which is before you!" It seemed to be my message for the day, so I repeated again and again, "Look with wonder at that which is before you."

At about noon, a large sum of money was given me, which I had been desiring for a certain purpose.

In a following chapter, I will give affirmations that I have found most effective. However, one should never use an affirmation unless it is absolutely satisfying and convincing to his own consciousness, and often an affirmation is changed to suit different people.

For example: The following has brought success to many: "I have wonderful work, in a wonderful way, I give wonderful service, for wonderful pay!"

I gave the first two lines to one of my students, and she added the last two.

It made a *most powerful statement,* as there should always be perfect payment for perfect service, and a rhyme sinks easily into the subconscious. She went about singing it aloud and soon did receive wonderful work in a wonderful way, and gave wonderful service for wonderful pay.

Another student, a businessman, took it and changed the word work to business. He repeated, "I have a wonderful business, in a wonderful way, and I give wonderful service for wonderful pay." That afternoon he made a forty-one thousand dollar deal, though there had been no activity in his affairs for months.

Every affirmation must be carefully worded and completely "cover the ground."

For example: I knew a woman who was in great need, and made a demand for work. She received a great deal of work, but was never paid anything. She now knows to add, "Wonderful service for wonderful pay."

It is man's Divine Right to have plenty! More than enough!

"His barns should be full, and his cup should flow over!" This is God's idea for man, and when man breaks down the barriers of lack in his own consciousness, the Golden Age will be his, and every righteous desire of his heart fulfilled!

WORKBOOK SESSION FOUR

The Law of Non-Resistance

Topics:

- Healing to Change

- Toxic Words and Thoughts

- The Law of Attraction

- Success Versus Failure — Adversity Versus-Golden Opportunity

- The Reasoning Mind Versus Reality

- Living in the Moment

- Affirmations and Expectancy

- Recap and Personal Journal

Begin this session by breathing deeply to achieve balance. Surround yourself with God's Divine White Light of Protection and set your intention to connect with your Higher Self.

Father, Mother, God, Creator of All That Is…

I claim my personal power and open the way to see clearly my Field of Potentiality, my field of infinite possibilities. I cut the ties of beliefs and thought patterns that no longer serve me in all directions of time, removing them from my consciousness, my subconscious, and my superconscious. I fearlessly step into the magnificence of the true essence of who I am — One with God. I graciously accept all that is mine by Divine Right, under grace in a miraculous way and commit to fulfill all that I came to be, have, and do in this incarnation on Mother Earth at this time.

Amen

Ask your guides, angels, and teachers to be present with you to help you open your heart, mind, and spirit to the infinite possibilities of you.

HEALING TO CHANGE

In Chapter 4 we're introduced to shifting our BE-ingness from the energy of "resistant" based in fear to "non-resistant" based in love. The state of being non-resistant is of love source and is All Powerful!

Fear is an illusion. The source of evil is fear.

Florence states that "evil is a false law man has made for himself, through soul sleep. "She defines Soul Sleep as when "man's soul has been hypnotized by the race belief (of sin, sickness, death) that is carnal or mortal thought, and his affairs have outpictured his illusions."

Let's put this statement into twenty-first century terminology. Soul sleep means "We have surrendered to the physical world teachings of hereditary illness, judgment, lack, and limitation and created an abundance of lack, illness, poverty, and sadness as our reality." An example of this is: "The sick man has pictured sickness, the poor man poverty, and the rich man wealth."

In the following Inside Assignments you will be asked to stand back as an observer and evaluate unhappy life situations and shift and heal the resistant fear to non-resistant love. Keep the following questions in mind, "Are you seeing where your thought processes based in fear source created the unhappy situation?" and "Were you able to discern what your mindset was prior to the creation of the situation?"

As you've worked through this workbook, you've been identifying fear and releasing it. As you grow and evolve, more fear may be revealed involving a situation you've already released. It is a clear sign that you're ascending in your love consciousness. So instead of being upset at discovering more fear, rejoice that it has been revealed to you. The reality is that finding more fear to heal is — a really good thing!

We must remember that non-resistance is NOT the path of least resistance. The "path of least resistance" is an external path. "Non-resistance" is internal. It is active faith that all is in Divine Order.

Toxic Words and Thoughts

The energy of thoughts and words is POWERFUL ENERGY!

If we would hold our children and those we love in the light of Powerful Master Creators instead of holding them in the darkness of fear and worry, how would their lives be different? When we hold those we love in "worry" we are sending negative energy to them. Sending out negative energy goes against Universal Law and has negative repercussions for all! Not only are we sending out worry energy to others, we're also planting "worry seeds" for ourselves that will grow and come back to us. Understanding Universal Laws is the key to harnessing our power. We are able to step fully into our power when we shift to love source and use the Universal Laws for our highest good.

Florence teaches us "Man who is centered and established in right thinking, the man who sends out only goodwill to his fellow man, and who is without fear, cannot be touched or influenced by the negative thoughts of others."

It is easy to take in the negativity of others.

The question is, are we "centered and established" in right thinking on a daily basis?

When we reconnect fully with our source, the Divinity or Higher Self within, we know that there is no evil. We will have experienced from within the true one power, God, and we will understand we are One with Him.

Florence teaches us that "carnal or mortal thought" (physical world conditioning) takes over our subconscious and , convincing us that fear is "normal." This makes us feel separate from God, the essence of who we are and we feel lost and confused.

If we must put a face to Evil, it is physical world conditioning of fear.

We know from our own lives that we have taken these teachings and allowed them to "outpicture" the Higher Self within us. We prove this by manifesting lack to the point of poverty as well as other forms of fearful situations. If there is a part of our Square of Life that is less than what we desire, it is because we have *allowed* the physical world conditionings of fear to control us.

It is our job, our Soul Purpose, to heal within and step into our Power in love source energy — One with God.

The Law of Attraction

We have learned that our thoughts, words, and actions are what create the reality of our lives. What we continually think about we become a magnet for. As we grow and develop on our spiritual journey, we will find that we become magnets for like-minded people. They will find us in amazing ways. Just as when we work in tandem with the three levels of consciousness, abundance that we desire will also find us in amazing ways.

In every moment we work with the Law of Attraction. We must monitor our thoughts so that they are based in love and gratitude — not fear — for if they are fear based, that is what we will be a magnet for: negativity and fear. Many people focus on what they don't want, then say the Law of Attraction doesn't work when they manifest something they don't want. The Law of Attraction worked perfectly, they simply used it to bring chaos, confusion, disharmony, and negativity into their lives. We are constantly in a ceaseless interaction of cause and effect. Through our thoughts, words, and beliefs we create the energy within us of love or of fear and we attract more of it to us — *all the time!* There are no time-outs!

In learning the Laws of the Universe, you are elevated to a higher level of understanding. It is up to you to utilize this information to the fullest extent possible.

INSIDE ASSIGNMENT

Minding Your Thoughts This exercise will bring to light the thoughts that sneak in and sabotage you. Sit quietly, and honestly look at your thought processes.

Identify a negative thought pattern or belief that you have.

Example: Do you get a cold every winter? In the recesses of your mind do you think, "I get a cold every winter"?

Write it down in the Negative Thought square. Then write about the negativity that has been attracted to you. Transmute it to positive. It may be necessary to use The Sedona Method® of Release or bonus gift "Shift Your Energy to Love" technique (www.Game-OfLifeMastery.com/freegift).

After you've examined how the Law of Attraction works with negative thoughts in your life, then examine it with positive thoughts. Think about your life and assess your thought patterns to discern which ones are positive. Identify the things that are attracted to you through the positive energy evoked from the thought pattern.

Fill in the Thought Patterns Form with your discoveries.

Do you now see the power of your thought processes? Use the Personal Journal Pages to write about your experience of the Law of Attraction.

SUCCESS VERSUS FAILURE — ADVERSITY VERSUS GOLDEN OPPORTUNITY

We live in a world of duality judgment. Our perception of life situations as successes or failures is based on this judgment. Florence shares with us the example of the man who claimed everything he did as "Success" even if by the judgment of the physical world it wasn't. In his mind he saw everything as success, therefore, it was.

In claiming everything as "Success" the man also invoked the Law of Attraction in a love-based positive way, attracting to him "Success!"

Thomas Edison did this. He tried thousands of times to create the light bulb. Each time his attempts didn't work he didn't feel like he failed; instead he regarded each attempt as having successfully pinpointed the methods that did not work. In his mind, he deemed what many would have judged a failure to be success. He stayed in love source and did not give up.

Through our free will we may choose to change our perception from the lower vibration of fear/failure to the higher vibration of love/success — as Thomas Edison did.

In this chapter, Florence uses the example of the woman who required money. The woman understood the spiritual law of opulence. She knew if she maintained a vibration of opulence she would *be a magnet for more feelings of opulence*. This is the Law of Attraction.

Then a man came into her life who talked of lack and limitation and she allowed her mindset and vibration to lower to his poverty level, then she *blamed him*. This is the typical human reaction, but it is victim mentality — and victim energy is FEAR! She gave all her power away by stepping into fear source.

Then she shifted her perspective and the man became the "golden link" or opportunity to understand how she was working against Universal Laws of prosperity abundance. The woman used her tools to dissolve her resistance (fear energy) and shift her energy to non-resistant love energy.

THOUGHT PATTERNS

Negative thought	Identify what you attracted
Positive thought	Identify what you attracted

Even though the man appeared to be a negative influence in her life, he was the catalyst for great prosperity for her. This was the perfection of the life situation. Her resistant feelings toward the man was her Golden Opportunity to look within to heal and ascend her low energetic vibration.

Every life situation holds perfection. It's easy to "see" the perfection in a good life situation, but difficult if we judge the situation as "bad." Perfection in seemingly adverse life situations provides the Golden Opportunity to heal within revealed by our inner feelings of resistance.

Previously you identified negative life situations or relationships and used The Sedona Method® of Release to transmute your fear to love. You did your best to transmute all the negative situations and relationships to a source of love and heal them. However, as a spiritual being experiencing a human existence you have two things that go on continually:

1. You live in a physical world in which daily life is laced with negative assaults to your spiritual being-ness.

2. You are now open to evolving and ascending to a higher level of consciousness, thereby revealing more and more layers of fear that must be addressed.

In transmuting the experience to positive energy from negative, you will find great peace and comfort. You will be free to move forward with your life at a higher vibration of love.

THE REASONING MIND VERSUS REALITY

Florence teaches us that in resisting a situation it will stay with us. If we run away from a situation, it will follow us. To drive this home, she uses the example of the woman who ran away from her critical, domineering mother and married a man just like her mother. She drew to her the exact same sit-uation she left because she ran from it instead of healing the energy within.

The "reasoning mind" would say, but the daughter's not the one who is critical and domineering, the mother is. Why should the daughter have to change? Remember Florence states, "unharmonious situations come from inharmony within man himself!" Relationships are all about us. The physical world teaches our "reasoning" mind that we are victims of the actions of others. But the truth is, we create our reality through our energy within — an unharmonious situation or relationship manifests as our reality from the Creation Energy within us.

The daughter created the unharmonious relationship with her mother. Because she maintained the inharmony (less than love) energy within her, she manifested another unharmonious relationship with her husband. Until the daughter claims her power by changing within, she will draw to herself over and over again, people who are critical and domineering.

Florence shares with us that people often came to her wanting her to "treat" for the people causing the adversity to change. Florence would refuse and say, "No, I will give treatments to change you!"

20 ▶ I N S I D E A S S I G N M E N T

Transmute to Love Look back at your day or week. Did anything happen that gave you that "angst" feeling in your chest? That tweak of "this isn't right" or "I don't like this" feeling? Identify one situation and write it in the Inharmonious Situation column. Then transmute the negativity of the situation to love-based feelings that leave you undisturbed.

Transmute the situation to achieve a non-emotional state by using The Sedona Method® of Release or the bonus gift "Shift Your Energy to Love" technique (www.GameOfLifeMastery.com/freegift).

When writing about your Inharmonious Situation focus on how the shift to love-source affects your experience.

NOTE: You must follow through and experience theprocesses of transforming the fear source energy to love or you will find yourself feeling confused and somewhat chaotic, held hostage by the less than love energy/fear revealed. Do the work of dissipating this fear with the exercises and journaling.

DISSIPATING INHARMONY

Inharmonious Situation	Energy Shift to Love Source — Harmony
_____	_____
_____	_____
_____	_____
_____	_____
_____	_____
_____	_____

LIVING IN THE MOMENT

Florence states: "The robbers of time are the past and the future. Man should bless the past and forget it and bless the future knowing it has in store for him endless joys, but live fully in the now."

Humans are notorious for dwelling, stewing, and worrying about the past and the future. Living in the past and worrying about the future is what we *do*. Living in the moment is something we miss.

The subconscious energy of creation only knows the moment of NOW — there is no past or future. Are you conscious "in the moment" of now?

In the next exercise you are asked to evaluate your day and distinguish the time you spent dwelling on the past, fretting about the future, living in the moment, and the really scary time spent on auto pilot in an oblivious state.

 21 INSIDE ASSIGNMENT

Here and Now This exercise will open your eyes to how much real time you spend living in the moment. Look back honestly at your day. Was there a time you were fretting about something that happened in the past? If so, jot it down in the Past column.

Next, determine if you were fretting or worrying about a future event. Be honest, this could be a future event concerning yourself or the world in general. Write about this in the Future column.

Evaluate your thoughts from the day to determine if there was any time spent experiencing the now, or In the Moment. Did you notice how blue the sky was? Did you breathe deeply and feel your lungs? If you remember doing anything that made you consciously remember the moment, write about it in the In the Moment column.

Now it gets interesting. How many moments during the day were you going through the motions oblivious to what you were doing? Do you remember the drive home? Do you remember showering? Do you remember feeling alive today? If you experienced this, be honest and write it down in the Oblivious column.

In honestly reviewing your daily life, it will become clear when your Creation Energy is unfocused — without supervision. Use the Journal Page to write about your discoveries.

LIVING IN THE MOMENT

Past	Future	In The Moment	Oblivious

AFFIRMATIONS AND EXPECTANCY

Florence states that "it is most necessary to begin the day with right words." She is reminding us that we bring into our lives what we think of. If we begin the day with negative thoughts, then that is what we are a magnet for. We will manifest negativity, chaos, and possibly disaster.

A clear example: I stayed with some friends before moving to Colorado. It was my job to waken the children for elementary school. Each morning I would go to their room and rouse them from sleep, telling them what a wonderful day they were going to have. The son was always quite grumpy and one day belligerent as well. Becoming frustrated, I told him, without thinking, that his day would be miserable and left the room. Granted, this was really a terrible thing to do, but the results were amazing. That evening when I got home from work, both of them came to me begging me to never tell them they would have a miserable day — for indeed, it had been. The son was very sorry for his grumpiness and would never behave like that again. And he didn't.

This example teaches us:

1. The children were not in control of the three levels of their consciousness, so they were easily influenced. Their subconscious record was written for the day by my words. We DO influence others, especially children, so we must be careful that our influence is based in love, not negativity.

2. Words are powerful. The statement "your day will be miserable" affirmed the day they would have — and they did.

Affirmations create expectancy of what is to come and anchors your faith in the receipt. The key to using affirmations is that they must "click" or resonate in your truth center to be powerful. As we read an affirmation, we know whether or not it resonates within us. Affirmation doctor, Dr. Anne

Marie Evers, author of *Affirmations, Your Passport to Happiness!*, states "Affirmations when properly done always work!"

When you feel that warm fuzzy glow within when reading an affirmation, USE IT. Your three levels of consciousness are in alignment! You are feeling the acknowledgment of the subconscious that it believes the affirmation — it is written in your record. As we have learned, if it is written in our subconscious record, the subconscious/Universe will work to bring it to fruition in our reality.

 INSIDE ASSIGNMENT

My Affirmations Affirmations are only powerful when they resonate or click deep within you. Using affirmations that click with you help to shift your energy and elevate you to the feeling of opulence.

The Affirmations Form lists a few affirmations. Read through each one and jot down, in the space under the affirmation, the feelings generated by the affirmation. Did the affirmation "click"? Or did it leave you flat? Rewrite the affirmation to fit your needs. Then write out a few affirmations of your own that resonate or click with you.

Write an affirmation for each area of your Square of Life for something you wish to create in that area. Make sure it clicks! Repeat it often — put it on a sticky note of the bathroom mirror, the fridge, and your computer monitor. Put it in places to remind you.

Integrating the daily use of powerful affirmations into your life will help you maintain living from a source of love. Use the Personal Journal to write about your experience using the affirmations.

AFFIRMATIONS

God is my supply. Money comes to me easily in unexpected ways by Divine Right and under grace.

I give thanks for this day, miracle shall follow miracle and wonders shall never cease.

I am an irresistible magnet for all that belongs to me by Divine Right.

I have wonderful work, in a wonderful way, I give wonderful service, for wonderful pay! With excellent benefits!

NOTE: If you're using an affirmation and suddenly it no longer "clicks" with you, look within to discern why. You may have ascended to a higher level of understanding and enlightenment and there is a fear to face and shift to love.

Bonus tool: Soul Kisses are spiritual affirmations received daily in your email. If you would like to receive them, please click in to SoulKisses.com.

RECAP

Each one of us has given our power away. We're taught to give our power away to others, to follow the leader and trust what others say without question. Reclaiming our power is a process. What we're learning through Florence's teachings is to look within and discern for ourselves what resonates with our truth center. At times the teachings seem complicated and a lot to do and take in, but the bottom line is simple: live in love source instead of fear.

What is tricky and sometimes complicated is discerning what is of love source and what is of fear source. The best way to tell the difference is to discern if resistance is involved. Resistance is of fear source. When we evaluate the resistance we're able to resolve it and shift our energy from fear to love.

Florence tells us that "it is man's Divine Right to have plenty! More than enough! His barns should be full, and his cup should flow over! This is God's idea for man." She has explained to us throughout the chapters that "when man breaks down the barriers of lack in his own consciousness, the Golden Age will be his, and every righteous desire of his heart fulfilled!"

Getting our minds around the fact that the prosperous abundance we desire is available to us can be challenging due to the teachings of the physical world. It is up to us to cast aside these teachings and look to discover and discern the Higher Self within, the superconscious mind, and to rewrite the records of our subconscious with our findings and monitor the thought patterns, beliefs, and words of our conscious.

Each one of us has a Field of Potentiality that holds all that we dream of. It is our choice to use tools to dissipate our feelings of unworthiness and living from a source of fear to stepping into our power and living from a source of love. It is then that we will have eliminated the blocks that prevent us from receiving the abundance we desire.

This chapter, The Law of Non-Resistance, is full of exciting information. The exercises require us to look at our lives in cold, hard honesty. If you look closely, you will see the changes you've made in your life from the knowledge in the previous chapters and see that you have, indeed, made great progress.

You will also see the healing that has begun. As we discussed before, as babies we are conditioned to fear, to believe we are limited and to doubt God's love for us. The writings of Florence Scovel Shinn not only help us to walk away from physical world conditioning, they also open the door to healing the pain we have experienced.

The information in this chapter alone will guide you to a stress-free pathway of living. When the mind gets around transmutation of negativity to a source of love, the doors to endless possibilities are opened. Frivolous worries of the past dissipate, leaving you free to enjoy simply breathing, while practicing living in the moment opens your eyes to true love and life.

You will find that your connection with God has grown tremendously. Look back at your life before you opened this workbook. In your mind's eye, travel through your growth. Miraculous, isn't it?

Again we've addressed "blessing your enemy and you rob him of his ammunition." The intention of blessing someone you feel threatened by shifts you from powerless to powerful, because there is no fear in love blessings.

Love is all-powerful.

Love dissolves resistance.

Love heals.

Now you have tools to help you maintain balance instead of feeling scattered and flustered. Use these tools and you will find your days less stressful and your life more joyous!

Be sure to use the Personal Journal section at the end of each session. Be good to yourself and write in them at least ten minutes each day about the things you are discovering, learning, and experiencing. As you do this, you will find elation living in your chest — it is the gift of love found in living in the palm of God. You will discover you are moving into a state of receiving avalanches of prosperity in all things.

Be sure to thank your angelic entourage for being in attendance and helping you to clearly understand God's work.

May you be profoundly blessed in this moment and in every moment after.

PERSONAL JOURNAL

_____

_____

_____

_____

_____

_____

_____

_____

_____

_____

_____

PERSONAL JOURNAL

CHAPTER 5

The Law of Karma and The Law of Forgiveness

■ ■ ■ ■ ■

Man receives only that which he gives. The Game of Life is a game of boomerangs. Man's thoughts, deeds, and words return to him sooner or later, with astounding accuracy.

This is the law of Karma, which is Sanskrit for "comeback." "Whatsoever a man soweth, that shall he also reap."

For example: A friend told me this story of herself, illustrating the law. She said, "I make all my Karma on my aunt, whatever I say to her, someone says to me. I am often irritable at home, and one day said to my aunt, who was talking to me during dinner, *'No more talk, I wish to eat in peace.'*

"The following day, I was lunching with a woman with whom I wished to make a great impression. I was talking animatedly, when she said: *'No more talk, I wish to eat in peace!'*"

My friend is high in consciousness, so her Karma returns much more quickly than to one on the mental plane.

The more man knows, the more he is responsible for, and a person with a knowledge of Spiritual Law, which he does not practice, suffers greatly in consequence. "The fear of the Lord (law) is the beginning of wisdom." If we read the word Lord, law, it will make many passages in the Bible much clearer.

"Vengeance is mine, I will repay saith the Lord (law)." It is the law which takes vengeance, not God. God sees man perfect, "created in his own image (imagination)" and given "power and dominion."

This is the perfect idea of man, registered in Divine Mind, awaiting man's recognition; for man can only be what he sees himself to be, and only attain what he sees himself attaining.

"Nothing ever happens without an onlooker" is an ancient saying.

Man sees first his failure or success, his joy or sorrow, before it swings into visibility from the scenes set in his own imagination. We have observed this in the mother picturing disease for her child, or a woman seeing success for her husband.

Jesus Christ said, "And ye shall know the truth and the truth shall make you free."

So, we see freedom (from all unhappy conditions) comes through knowledge, a knowledge of Spiritual Law.

Obedience precedes authority, and the law obeys man when he obeys the law. The law of electricity must be obeyed before it becomes man's servant. When handled ignorantly, it becomes man's deadly foe. *So with the laws of Mind!*

For example: A woman with a strong personal will wished she owned a house that belonged to an acquaintance, and she often made mental pictures of herself living in the house. In the course of time, the man died and she moved into the house. Several years afterward, coming into the knowledge of Spiritual Law, she said to me: "Do you think I had anything to do with that man's death?" I replied: "Yes, your desire was so strong, everything made way for it, but you paid your Karmic debt. Your husband, whom you loved devotedly, died soon after, and the house was a white elephant on your hands for years."

The original owner, however, could not have been affected by her thoughts had he been positive in the truth, nor her husband, but they were both under Karmic law. The woman should have said (feeling the great desire for the house), "Infinite Intelligence, give me the right house, equally as charming as this, the house *which is mine by Divine Right.*"

The divine selection would have given perfect satisfaction and brought good to all. The divine pattern is the only safe pattern to work by.

Desire is a tremendous force, and must be directed in the right channels, or chaos ensues.

In demonstrating, the most important step is the *first step, to "ask aright."*

Man should always demand only that which is his by *Divine Right.*

To go back to the illustration: Had the woman taken this attitude: "If this house, I desire, is mine, I cannot lose it, if it is not, give me its equivalent," the man might have decided to move out, harmoniously (had it been the divine selection for her) or another house would have been substituted. Anything forced into manifestation through personal will is always "ill-got," and has "ever bad success."

Man is admonished, "My will be done not thine," and the curious thing is, man always gets just what he desires when he does relinquish personal will, thereby enabling Infinite Intelligence to work through him.

"Stand ye still and see the salvation of the Lord (law)."

For example: A woman came to me in great distress. Her daughter was determined to take a very hazardous trip, and the mother was filled with fear.

She said she had used every argument, had pointed out the dangers to be encountered, and forbidden her to go, but the daughter became more and more rebellious and determined. I said to the mother, "You are forcing your personal will upon your daughter, which you have no right to do, and your fear of the trip is only attracting it, for man attracts what he fears." I added, "Let go, and take your mental hands off; *put it in God's Hands, and use this statement:* 'I put this situation in the hands of Infinite Love and Wisdom; if this trip is the Divine plan, I bless it and no longer resist, but if it is not divinely planned, I give thanks that it is now dissolved and dissipated.'"

A day or two after that, her daughter said to her, "Mother, I have given up the trip," and the situation returned to its "native nothingness."

It is learning to "stand still," which seems so difficult for man. I have dealt more fully with this law in the chapter on non-resistance.

I will give another example of sowing and reaping, which came in the most curious way.

A woman came to me saying she had received a counterfeit twenty-dollar bill, given to her at the bank. She was much disturbed, for, she said, "the people at the bank will never acknowledge their mistake."

I replied, "Let us analyze the situation and find out why you attracted it." She thought a few moments and exclaimed: "I know it, I sent a friend a lot of stage money, just for a joke." So the law had sent her some stage money, for it doesn't know anything about jokes.

I said, "Now we will call on the law of forgiveness, and neutralize the situation."

Christianity is founded upon the law of forgiveness — Christ has redeemed us from the curse of the Karmic law, and the Christ within each man is his Redeemer and Salvation from all inharmonious conditions.

So I said: "Infinite Spirit, we call on the law of forgiveness and give thanks that she is under grace and not under law, and cannot lose this twenty dollars which is hers by Divine Right."

"Now," I said, "go back to the bank and tell them, fearlessly, that it was given you there by mistake."

She obeyed, and to her surprise, they apologized and gave her another bill, treating her most courteously.

So knowledge of the Law gives man power to "rub out his mistakes." Man cannot force the external to be what he is not.

If he desires riches, he must be rich first in consciousness.

For example: A woman came to me asking treatment for prosperity. She did not take much interest in her household affairs, and her home was in great disorder.

I said to her, "If you wish to be rich, you much be orderly. All men with great wealth are orderly — and order is heaven's first law." I added, "You will never become rich with a burnt match in the pin cushion."

She had a good sense of humor and commenced immediately, putting her house in order. She rearranged furniture, straightened out bureau drawers, cleaned rugs, and soon made a big financial demonstration: a gift from a relative. The woman, herself, became made over, and keeps herself keyed-up financially, by being ever watchful of the *external and expecting prosperity, knowing God is her supply.*

Many people are in ignorance of the fact that gifts and things are investments, and that hoarding and saving invariably lead to loss.

"There is that scattereth and yet increaseth; and there is that withholdeth more than is meet, but it tendeth to poverty."

For example: I knew a man who wanted to buy a fur-lined overcoat. He and his wife went to various shops, but there was none he wanted. He said they were all too cheap-looking. At last, he was shown one that, the salesman said was valued at a thousand dollars, but which the manager would sell to him for five hundred dollars, as it was late in the season.

His financial possessions amounted to about seven hundred dollars. The reasoning mind would have said, "You can't afford to spend nearly all you have on a coat," but he was very intuitive and never reasoned.

He turned to his wife and said, "If I get this coat, I'll make a ton of money!" So his wife consented, weakly.

About a month later, he received a ten-thousand-dollar commission. The coat made him feel so rich, it linked him with success and prosperity; without the coat he would not have received the commission. It was an investment paying large dividends!

If man ignores these leadings to spend or to give, the same amount of money will go in an uninteresting or unhappy way.

For example: A woman told me, on Thanksgiving Day, she informed her family that they could not afford a Thanksgiving dinner. She had the money, but decided to save it.

A few days later, someone entered her room and took from the bureau drawer the exact amount the dinner would have cost.

The law always stands back of the man who spends fearlessly, with wisdom.

For example: One of my students was shopping with her little nephew. The child clamored for a toy, which she told him she could not afford to buy for him.

She realized suddenly that she was seeking lack, and not recognizing God as her supply!

So she bought the toy, and on her way home, picked up, in the street, *the exact amount of money she had paid for it.*

Man's supply is inexhaustible and unfailing when fully trusted, but faith or trust must precede the demonstration. "According to your faith be it unto you." "Faith is the substance of things hoped for, the evidence of things not seen," for faith holds the vision steady, and the adverse pictures are dissolved and dissipated, and "in due season we shall reap, if we faint not."

Jesus Christ brought the good news (the gospel) that there was a higher law than the law of Karma, and that that law transcends the law of Karma. It is the law of grace, or forgiveness. It is the law that *frees man from the law of cause and effect, the law of consequence. "Under grace, and not under law."*

We are told that on this plane, man reaps where he has not sown; the gifts of God are simply poured out upon him. "All that the Kingdom affords is his." This continued state of bliss awaits the man who has overcome the race (or world) thought.

In the world thought there is tribulation, but Jesus Christ said: "Be of good cheer; I have overcome the world."

The world thought is that of sin, sickness, and death. He saw their absolute unreality and said sickness and sorrow shall pass away, and death itself, the last enemy, be overcome.

We know now, from a scientific standpoint, that death could be overcome by stamping the subconscious mind with the conviction of eternal youth and eternal life.

The subconscious, being simply power without direction, *carries out orders without questioning.*

Working under the direction of the superconscious (the Christ or God within man) the "resurrection of the body" would be accomplished.

Man would no longer throw off his body in death, it would be transformed into the "body electric," sung by Walt Whitman, for Christianity is founded upon the forgiveness of sins and "an empty tomb."

WORKBOOK SESSION FIVE

The Law of Karma and The Law of Forgiveness

Topics:

- The Law of Karma

- Visualization — a Manifestation Skill

- Divine Right and Asking Aright

- Control and Non-Resistance

- The Law of Forgiveness

- The Energy of Money

- Our Supply Is Inexhaustible and Unfailing

- Overcoming Physical World Conditioning

- Recap and Personal Journal

Begin this session by breathing deeply to achieve balance. Surround yourself with God's Divine White Light of Protection and set your intention to connect with your Higher Self.

Father, Mother, God, Creator of All That Is…

I claim my personal power and open the way to see clearly my Field of Potentiality, my field of infinite possibilities. I cut the ties of beliefs and thought patterns that no longer serve me in all directions of time, removing them from my consciousness, my subconscious, and my superconscious. I fearlessly step into the magnificence of the true essence of who I am — One with God. I graciously accept all that is mine by Divine Right, under grace in a miraculous way and commit to fulfill all that I came to be, have, and do in this incarnation on Mother Earth at this time.

Amen

Ask your guides, angels, and teachers to be present with you to help you open your heart, mind, and spirit to the infinite possibilities of you.

THE LAW OF KARMA

In Chapter 5, The Law of Karma and The Law of Forgiveness, we delve more deeply into the power of our words as seeds planting the experiences of our lives. Florence explains to us that karma is the return of man's thoughts, deeds, and words, they "return to him sooner or later with astounding accuracy — like boomerangs." She describes karma as "Whatsoever a man soweth, that shall he also reap" and gives the example of the woman who wasn't nice to her aunt by telling her to "be quiet, she wished to eat," then experiencing the same thing done to her by a woman she wished to impress.

Florence stated: "My friend is high in consciousness, so her karma returns to her much more quickly than to one on the mental plane." This was the case in 1925 when Florence self-published *The Game of Life,* but things have changed since that time.

Due to the active changes in the vibration of the energy of our planet, the veil that delayed the return of karma and the manifestation of our focus is dissolving. Karma is returning quickly whether one is of high consciousness or not. *And the creation of what we focus our thoughts and energy on is manifesting as our reality more quickly than ever before.*

The old paradigm of living in the veil of darkness without knowledge of spiritual law and still living an unawakened but happy life is over. Many of our basic belief structures are being challenged and are dissipating. We are experiencing the end of the paradigm of life as we have known it for centuries.

Some would say they wish to "opt out" of this experience, but no one has a choice. Ascending love energy flooding Mother Earth is affecting each one of us — no matter who you are, your physical and spiritual bodies are making the effort to align with these new energies.

Yet we do have a choice. We can go kicking and screaming, battered and bruised, into this new energetic frequency of Christ Consciousness, or we can embrace these changes and flow with ease and grace into this new paradigm using the tools presented to us by Florence in 1925.

Our Soul Purpose as a human on Mother Earth is to shift from the energy of fear-based illusion to that of love. We are here to raise our vibrational frequency to that of love and stepping into our power.

When we as individuals heal within, we send out a ripple effect across the planet, touching others AND Mother Earth with healing love. As you come to understand the new paradigm of living, each one of you will be teachers for those who are searching for tools to dissipate the false feeling of separation from God that is taught by the physical world.

Anyone who has been successful in the past will tell you that the old paradigm of creating what you want was to discern what you desire, create a plan of action steps to achieve it, and just do it. The energy of the planet no longer supports this way of living — it no longer works.

The new paradigm of living is to discern what you desire to be, do, or have, identify the resistance (which is fear) within, use your tools to disconnect from and heal that fear. Then shift into the energy of what it would feel like to receive what you desire and take action steps (if there are any) that you are guided to take.

The fluctuation of energy that the earth is experiencing is at a much higher vibration of love source than ever before.

Each one of us has the power to manifest our thoughts into our reality instantly, and that time is upon us. What we must be mindful of is that the Universe doesn't make a distinction between our creating a thought of something we want or something we don't want — it simply matches energy for energy. If we're "thinking" about something we don't want, we're giving energy to it. Remember the Universe does not recognize the meaning of NOT. So we must focus our "thought" energy on what we want — at the highest vibration we are capable of to draw to us that of our highest good.

Look honestly at your life. Do you see how you attract/create negative results for yourself? Do you see how you attract/create good/positive results for yourself?

 INSIDE ASSIGNMENT

Where Did This Come From? Write about several situations for which you created bad karma for yourself. Then write out several situations for which you created good karma for yourself. Go back to the bad karma and consider ways to change and/or neutralize it. You may discover that there is work to do within to change the behavior or feelings that created the bad karma. Use the tools you've learned to make the change.

Use the Personal Journal to write about the behaviors you have discovered in evaluating your creation of bad and good karma. This exercise provides insight into the things we do subconsciously, without thinking. Once you have identified negative thought patterns and/or beliefs, you have the tools to change them and move to a much happier life path.

BAD KARMA   **GOOD KARMA**

_____   _____

_____   _____

_____   _____

_____   _____

_____   _____

_____   _____

_____   _____

_____   _____

_____   _____

_____   _____

_____   _____

_____   _____

VISUALIZATION — A MANIFESTATION SKILL

Many of us live our lives going through the motions of living life. We don't get clear on what we want to do or what we want to accomplish.

Visualization is a powerful manifestation skill. By visualizing we write the record of receipt in our subconscious.

Florence reminds us of this in the examples from previous chapters of the woman who pictured disease manifesting in her child and a woman seeing success for her husband. These things were visualized first — written into the subconscious record and manifested into reality. Notice that one of the examples is negative and one is positive. Coming into knowledge of spiritual law will help us to eliminate manifesting things we don't want.

As children we "make believe" as we play, for we have no limits in imagination. As adults, we must call on these skills of unrestricted, clear thinking to reach deep within ourselves to discern what we truly desire — what is ours by Divine Right — what is ours in our Field of Potentiality. God has great abundance for us.

In getting our minds around and flexing our ability to visualize what we want to receive, what we want to do, what we want to be, or what we want to accomplish, we find ourselves truly limitless. In God all things are possible.

When we visualize ourselves experiencing something, our visualization sets the Universe into motion to manifest our vision into our lives. Remember this is whatever we are visualizing ourselves doing — things we do want as well as things we do NOT want.

 INSIDE ASSIGNMENT

Visual Receipt   Determine one thing that you desire. Write what it is under the Thank You, God, for: column. Can you visualize receiving it? Can you reach a feeling of elation of opulence due to having received it? Write about it under the Visualize Receipt column.

Use the Personal Journal to write about your discoveries. Is it easy or difficult for you to discern what you desire? Is it easy or difficult for you to visualize? If it is difficult, why? Do you have lingering feelings of unworthiness? Use your tools to be rid of unworthy feelings.

VISUALIZATION

Thank You, God, for: **Visualize Receipt**

_____   _____

_____   _____

_____   _____

_____   _____

_____   _____

_____   _____

_____   _____

_____   _____

_____   _____

_____   _____

DIVINE RIGHT AND ASKING ARIGHT

As we grow and come into more knowledge of creating the lives we truly wish to live, we begin to wonder about not only "covering the ground," as Florence terms it, but also of asking for what we desire in the correct way AND if what we desire is really ours.

Florence states, "Desire is a tremendous force, and must be directed in the right channels, or chaos ensues."

She uses the example of the woman who wanted a house that belonged to someone else. The woman was able to purchase the house because the owner died, then when she received it, her husband died. The woman focused her energies on what she desired, the house, vibrated at the energy of the house, and the Universe brought it to her.

Had the woman looked within and evaluated the core of the feelings she had for the house, she would have discovered her desire was energy. Had she then focused on receipt of the energy, she would have then been non-resistant to receiving the house that was hers by "Divine Right" and she would have been guided to the house that matched her energy — the house that was in her Field of Potentiality. As Florence stated, it may have been the same house, but the outcome would have been more harmonious.

Fear was involved in the woman manifesting the house she desired. Florence noted that the man who originally owned the house who died and the woman's husband who died were of the lower vibration of fear, so the woman's fear energy was able to touch them.

Discerning if there is fear involved in what we want to be, do, and have are key to whether what we desire is in our Field of Potentiality or not. This concept is a little tricky. Following are question tools the woman could have used to discern if her desire for the house held fear:

1. Do I feel angst/resistance within me that someone else has something I want? Had the woman asked herself this, she may have discovered she didn't like the fact that someone else lived in "her house."

2. Am I willing to receive something that is equivalent to what I desire? Being willing to receive something equivalent or better opens the way for the Universe to bring to us something even better than what we originally desired, plus we are non-resistant to the situation, because we've shifted into love source knowing what we desire is ours.

3. Do I see it in my Field of Potentiality? As we learn to "see" what is in our Field of Potentiality we will recognize if something we "think" we want is in there or not.

This brings up another point in regard to our Field of Potentiality. Often times our heart yearns for something, and we feel we aren't worthy to receive our desire, so we're willing to "settle" for something else.

What we yearn for **is in** our Field of Potentiality, what we "settle" for is not. So we must remember there is no happiness or joy in what we "settle" for. We can match our energy to and draw into our reality exactly what is in our Field of Potentiality and we must hold out for it. Settling for something outside the Field opens us up to heartache and disappointment, just like forcing things into manifestation.

When we are in love source and we state we "want" something, it is a command that kicks the Universe into action of leading us to that which we desire.

CONTROL AND NON-RESISTANCE

People have a hard time relinquishing control of relationships, situations, and conditions. We want to control everything. By holding on to the need to control every aspect of our life and someone else's, we block the prosperity that is ours.

In relinquishing this need to control, we become non-resistant and draw to us what we desire. Florence uses the example of the woman whose daughter wanted to take a trip that would be hazardous. The woman forced her personal will on the daughter and forbade her to go through fear. The fear acted as a magnet and made the trip more attractive to the daughter. Florence told her: "Let go, and take your mental hands off; put it in God's Hands, and use this statement: I put this situation in the hands of Infinite Love and Wisdom; if this trip is the Divine plan, I bless it and no longer resist, but if it is not divinely planned, I give thanks that it is now dissolved and dissipated."

The affirmation blessed the situation (we've learned how powerful blessing a person and/or situation is) and she gave thanks for the plans being dissolved even though there was no dissolution in site.

Letting go of worry and giving things to God or the Universe to handle takes a lot of faith and trust. As humans it is our pattern to give things to God, then take them back and play with them. This is called worry.

In the previous example Florence pointed out to the mother that she was "forcing her personal will" on the daughter. This is what we do, as humans — we "force our personal will" on others. Most of the time we do it out of love for others, like this mother and her daughter, but it is still "forcing our personal will" on others.

What we must realize is that we each come here with our path to experience. We may not agree with the paths of those we love, but it is their paths to experience. If we don't allow them to experience the path of their choice, they are denied the growth that they came here to experience.

The words transmuted the woman's fear to feelings of love-based non-resistance, thereby dissipating the fear. The magnetic pull of the fear vanished. Florence helped the mother to shift from a state of fear source to non-resistant love source by helping her remove her mental hands from the situation and allowing God to handle it. What a POWERFUL shift of energy!

The three levels of consciousness were working in tandem once again. The conscious mind stated the affirmation. The superconscious mind trusted God to handle the situation, and the subconscious mind's record was rewritten from one of fear, to one of non-resistance. Trust shifted the mother to a state of love.

 INSIDE ASSIGNMENT

Free Will This exercise is designed to evaluate your ability to use your free will wisely by working in tandem with God — practicing non-resistance.

Review the form. In the Situation/Event columns write in a situation/event that has taken place before and since you've been working in this workbook. Evaluate your actions. Did you work with God and allow His will to be done, or did you try to handle everything on your own? What was the end result? Write your actions in the appropriate column.

Use the Personal Journal to write about your discoveries. What happened before you had the tools in the workbook? How did you implement your tools to achieve non-resistance? Are you seeing that everything you do is a choice? Are you understanding the power of non-resistance?

FREE WILL AND NON-RESISTANCE

Situation/Event BEFORE This Workbook

My Reaction

_____

_____

_____

_____

_____

_____

_____

_____

_____

_____

_____

_____

Situation/Event DURING This Workbook

My Reaction

_____

_____

_____

_____

_____

_____

_____

_____

_____

_____

THE LAW OF FORGIVENESS

"Jesus Christ taught that there was a higher law than the law of karma — and that that law transcends the law of karma. It is the law of grace or forgiveness. It is the law which frees man from the law of cause and effect — the law of consequence. Under grace and not under law."

Florence states that "Christ has redeemed us from the curse of the karmic law, and the Christ within each man is his Redeemer and Salvation from all inharmonious conditions."

Through the Law of Attraction we become magnetized to the energy frequencies we put out to the Universe. If our energy is negative, we become a magnet for negative experiences: bad karma. If we transmute our negativity to a basis of love, we become a magnet for loving experiences: good karma/love.

Florence gives an outstanding example of the Universe and subconscious not having a sense of humor when she shares with us the story of the woman who gave someone stage money and received a counterfeit twenty dollar bill from the bank.

The Universe has no sense of humor, nor does the subconscious mind, as we have learned.

This doesn't mean we can't have fun anymore, but instead opens our eyes to the reality of the power of our thoughts, words, and actions.

Having realized she had received a counterfeit twenty, the woman immediately went into fear energy. To neutralize the situation, Florence invoked the Law of Forgiveness. She "treated" for the woman and shifted her into love source to receive what was "rightfully" hers.

Forgiveness is love source energy and rewrites our subconscious record, stopping the negative from manifesting. The negative is replaced with love and harmony, making us a magnet for only love, and fear is eradicated.

When we forgive others, we transmute our feelings from feelings based in fear to feelings based in love. This raises our vibrational frequency of energy to love, notifying the Universal Supply Warehouse to "match" love-based people, things, and situations to us.

When we *forgive ourselves — our actions, thoughts, beliefs and others —* we transmute more feelings from fear to love. Remember EVERYTHING is either love based or fear based — there is no in between. After forgiving ourselves, our energy frequency is raised to an even higher vibration to attract even higher prosperity.

Note: Forgiving others does not condone bad behavior. Forgiving others heals fear within us and shifts our energy to love source.

 26   INSIDE ASSIGNMENT

Forgiveness This exercise is designed to help you forgive, raising your vibrational frequency, which you a magnet for higher vibrational desires. Look honestly at your life. Write about an event/person you need to forgive under the Situation/Event/Relationship column. You may use The Sedona Method of Release® to forgive. Write about the experience in the Forgiveness Experience column.

Use the Personal Journal to write about what you discovered about yourself in this exercise. Were you able to forgive? Or do you still have that "angst" feeling in your chest or belly? Forgive yourself for your part in the event. Write about your experience.

FORGIVENESS

Situation/Event/Relationship

Forgiveness Experience

_____   _____

_____   _____

_____   _____

_____   _____

_____   _____

_____   _____

_____   _____

_____   _____

_____   _____

_____   _____

_____   _____

THE ENERGY OF MONEY

It seems that everywhere we go, the media is telling us that money solves our problems. As a result, we give money great power that makes us fearful of letting it go.

In shifting our mindset from the fear-based belief "money will solve my problems" to the love-based belief "money is only energy and I live in an abundant Universe with more than enough for me," our anxiousness and anxiety around money dissolves.

Florence uses the example of the man who shifted into the state of opulence when he purchased the coat that all but wiped out his finances. His shift into the state of opulence raised his vibration to match that of work that provided a large commission — the work resided in his Field of Potentiality.

The coat flooded the man with feelings of opulence, raising his vibration to that of love source, he trusted the feelings of his "truth center," let go of the money without fear, and attracted to him more feelings of opulence with the huge commission.

When we shift from fear source to love source and move into the state of knowing from deep within that we do indeed live in an abundant Universe and there is more than enough for each one of us, life changes. We shift our energy to love source all the way to our core being — back into the spiritual essence that is our light.

OUR SUPPLY IS INEXHAUSTIBLE AND UNFAILING

God is the true one and only power. God is limitless. His supply of abundance is inexhaustible and unfailing. God is the Universal Supply Warehouse.

We are limitless spiritual beings experiencing a human existence. As humans we limit ourselves through physical world conditioning, often times dissolving our dreams completely. Through this conditioning we also come to the belief that we are unworthy to receive good things.

When we are in love source, we dissipate these self-imposed limits both on ourselves and on God. We work together as one practicing trust and faith that God is our supply. It is through this partnership that we change our way of thinking and we rewrite our subconscious records to reflect the limitlessness of God and ourselves. In conjunction with the tools we are learning we achieve the feelings of opulence and expect prosperity, because we are prosperous from within. What is written in the subconscious mind within, manifests to the external — it is Universal Law.

OVERCOMING PHYSICAL WORLD CONDITIONING

Jesus Christ said, "Be of good cheer; I have overcome the world." Jesus understood that the spirit lives forever, that only the physical body dies. The physical world teaches that death is something to be feared, when in truth death is but a breath of transition from the physical world to the spiritual. Death is not to be feared, but to be honored.

Florence states that a "continued state of bliss awaits the man who has overcome the race (or world) thought." We've learned that this is true. We have learned through the workbook exercises that the teaching of the physical world, the conditioning, is a false power that is limited, negative, and destructive. The conditioning is a block between us and God, creating our feeling of separateness.

We've learned tools to overcome physical world conditioning. What we must understand is that we are still spirits experiencing a human existence. As humans we are susceptible to the continued conditioning of the physical world. It is up to us to daily monitor the effect the world has on our collective consciousness. It is up to us to use the tools we've learned to eradicate any negativity that is revealed to us or has made its way into our thought patterns or beliefs. In shaking off the physical world principles daily we are able to maintain our spiritual balance and alignment with the three levels of consciousness. Stress, worry, and fear become things of the past, and profound, prosperous abundance in the Square of Life becomes our daily routine — instead of a wish. We become a magnet for miracles.

RECAP

This chapter helps us become more aware of the cause and effect of our deeds, words, and thoughts. Our understanding becomes more complete about karma and how to neutralize what we unintentionally set into motion with the energy of our words and thoughts. We recognize now how visualization skills write our subconscious records and how to use that tool for our highest good.

By journaling and using the Inside Assignments we now know how to use the Universal Laws in a positive manner to bring to us what we desire instead of what we don't desire.

Deep within us we are becoming accustomed to the fact that God is our supply and that we are worthy of prosperity. Physical world conditioning does not stop over night. In addition, we are reintroduced to it on a daily basis by interacting with the outside world through internet, phone, television, radio, friends, family, etc. It is important that we monitor our words, thoughts, and deeds on a moment-to-moment basis during our daily lives in order to break the cycle. Maintaining a lifestyle free from negativity takes patience and diligence, yet the rewards are beyond measure. Practicing living from a foundation of love and working in tandem with the three levels of consciousness in balance are the keys to a fulfilled Square of Life.

Honor those around you. Honor yourself. Allow the Higher Self within to come out to play. Allow the Higher Self within to help you make decisions. Acknowledge the blessings that come to your life — graciously give thanks. Use the Personal Journal to write about the changes you are experiencing in your life. The more you allow yourself to have "the eyes to see," the more you will see!

The Universal Laws are just like the energy affecting the planet. No one gets to opt out. You've opened your heart, mind, and spirit to the knowledge of Universal Laws and you now have tools that make you unstoppable!

Be sure to thank your angelic entourage for being in attendance and helping you to clearly understand God's work.

May you be profoundly blessed in this moment and in every moment after.

PERSONAL JOURNAL

PERSONAL JOURNAL

CHAPTER 6

Casting the Burden

■ ■ ■ ■ ■

When man knows his own powers and the workings of his mind, his great desire is to find an easy and quick way to impress the subconscious with good, for simply an intellectual knowledge of the Truth will not bring results.

In my own case, I found the easiest way is in "casting the burden."

A metaphysician once explained it in this manner. He said, "The only thing which gives anything weight in nature, is the law of gravitation, and if a boulder could be taken high above the planet, there would be no weight in that boulder; and that is what Jesus Christ meant when he said: "My yoke is easy and my burden is light."

He had overcome the world vibration, and functioned in the fourth dimensional realm, where there is only perfection, completion, life and joy.

He said: "Come to me all ye that labor and are heavy laden, and I will give you rest." "Take my yoke upon you, for my yoke is easy and my burden is light."

We are also told in the fifty-fifth Psalm to "cast thy burden upon the Lord." Many passages in the Bible state that the *battle is God's* not man's and that man is always to *"stand still" and see the Salvation of the Lord.*

This indicates that the superconscious mind (or Christ within) is the department which fights man's battle and relieves him of burdens.

We see, therefore, that man violates law if he carries a burden, and a burden is an adverse thought or condition, and this thought or condition has its root in the subconscious.

_____

_____

_____

_____

_____

_____

_____

_____

_____

_____

_____

_____

_____

_____

It seems almost impossible to make any headway directing the subconscious from the conscious or reasoning mind, as the reasoning mind (the intellect) is limited in its conceptions, and filled with doubts and fears.

How scientific it then is, to cast the burden upon the superconscious mind (or Christ within) where it is "made light," or dissolved into its native nothingness."

For example: A woman in urgent need of money, "made light" upon the Christ within, the superconscious, with the statement, "I cast this burden of lack on the Christ (within) and I go free to have plenty!"

The belief in lack was her burden, and as she cast it upon the Superconscious with its belief of plenty, an avalanche of supply was the result.

We read, "The Christ in you the hope of glory."

Another example: One of my students had been given a new piano, and there was no room in her studio for it until she had moved out the old one. She was in a state of perplexity. She wanted to keep the old piano, but knew of no place to send it. She became desperate, as the new piano was to be sent immediately; in fact, was on its way, with no place to put it. She said it came to her to repeat, "I cast this burden on the Christ within, and I go free."

A few moments later, her phone rang, and a woman friend asked if she might rent her old piano, and it was moved out, a few minutes before the new one arrived.

I knew a woman whose burden was resentment. She said, "I cast this burden of resentment on the Christ within, and I go free, to be loving, harmonious and happy." The Almighty superconscious flooded the subconscious with love, and her whole life was changed. For years, resentment had held her in a state of torment and imprisoned her soul (the subconscious mind).

The statement should be made over and over and over, sometimes for hours at a time, silently or audibly, with quietness but determination.

I have often compared it to winding-up a victrola. We must wind ourselves up with spoken words.

I have noticed, in "casting the burden," after a little while, one seems to see clearly. It is impossible to have clear vision while in the throes of carnal mind. Doubts and fear poison the mind and body, and imagination runs riot, attracting disaster and disease.

In steadily repeating the affirmation, "I cast this burden on the Christ within, and go free," the vision clears, and with it a feeling of relief, and sooner or later comes *the manifestation of good, be it health, happiness, or supply.*

One of my students once asked me to explain the "darkness before the dawn." I referred in a preceding chapter to the fact that often, before the big demonstration, "everything seems to go wrong," and deep depression clouds the consciousness. It means that out of the subconscious are rising the doubts and fears of the ages. These old derelicts of the subconscious rise to the surface, *to be put out.*

It is then that man should clap his cymbals, like Jehoshaphat, and give thanks that he is saved, even though he seems surrounded by the enemy (the situation of lack or disease). The student continued, "How long must one remain in the dark," and I replied, "until one *can see in the dark,* and *"casting the burden enables one to see in the dark."*

In order to impress the subconscious, active faith is always essential.

"Faith without works is dead." In these chapters I have endeavored to bring out this point.

Jesus Christ showed active faith when "He commanded the multitude to sit down on the ground," before he gave thanks for the loaves and fishes.

I will give another example showing how necessary this step is. In fact, active faith is the bridge, over which man passes to his Promised Land.

Through misunderstanding, a woman had been separated from her husband, whom she loved deeply. He refused all offers of reconciliation and would not communicate with her in any way.

Coming into the knowledge of Spiritual law, she denied the appearance of separation. She made this statement: "There is no separation in Divine Mind, therefore, I cannot be separated form the love and companionship which are mine by Divine Right."

She showed active faith by arranging a place for him at the table every day; thereby impressing the subconscious with a picture of his *return.* Over a year passed, but she never wavered, and *one day he walked in.*

The subconscious is often impressed through music. Music has a fourth dimensional quality and releases the soul from imprisonment. It makes wonderful things seem *possible, and easy of accomplishment!*

I have a friend who uses her victrola, daily, for this purpose. It puts her in perfect harmony and releases the imagination.

_____

_____

_____

_____

_____

_____

_____

_____

_____

_____

_____

_____

_____

_____

Another woman often dances while making her affirmations. The rhythm and harmony of music and motion carry her words forth with tremendous power.

The student must remember also not to despise the "day of small things."

Invariably, before a demonstration, come "signs of land."

Before Columbus reached America, he saw birds and twigs, which showed him land was near. So it is with a demonstration; but often the student mistakes it for the demonstration itself, and is disappointed.

For example: A woman had "spoken the word" for a set of dishes. Not long afterwards a friend gave her a dish that was old and cracked.

She came to me and said, "Well, I asked for a set of dishes, and all I got was a cracked plate."

I replied, "The plate was only signs of land. It shows your dishes are coming — look upon it as birds and seaweed," and not long afterwards the dishes came.

Continually "making believe" impresses the subconscious. If one makes believe he is rich, and makes believe he is successful, in "due time he will reap."

Children are always "making believe," and "except ye be converted, and become as little chidren, ye shall not enter the Kingdom of Heaven."

For example: I know of a woman who was very poor, but no one could make her feel poor. She earned a small amount of money from rich friends, who constantly reminded her of her poverty, and to be careful and save. Regardless of their admonitions, she would spend all her earnings on a hat, or make someone a gift, and be in a rapturous state of mind. Her thoughts were always centered on beautiful clothes and "rings and things," but without envying others.

She lived in the world of the wondrous, and only riches seemed real to her. Before long she married a rich man, and the rings and things became visible. I do not know whether the man was the "Divine Selection," but opulence had to manifest in her life, as she had imaged only opulence.

There is no peace or happiness for man until he has erased all fear from the subconscious.

Fear is misdirected energy and must be redirected, or transmuted into Faith.

Jesus Christ said, "Why are ye fearful, O ye of little faith?" "All things are possible to him that believeth."

I am asked so often by my students, *"How can I get rid of fear?"*

I reply, *"By walking up to the thing you are afraid of."*

"The lion takes its fierceness from your fear."

Walk up to the lion, and he will disappear; run away and he runs after you.

I have shown in previous chapters how the lion of lack disappeared when the individual spent money fearlessly, showing faith that God was his supply and therefore, unfailing.

Many of my students have come out of the bondage of poverty, and are now bountifully supplied, through losing all fear of letting money go out. The subconscious is impressed with the truth that *God is the Giver and Gift*; therefore as one is one with the Giver, he is one with the Gift. A splendid statement is, "I now thank God the Giver for God the Gift."

Man has so long separated himself from his good and his supply through thoughts of separation and lack, that sometimes it takes dynamite to dislodge these false ideas from the subconscious, and the dynamite is a big situation.

We see in the foregoing illustration, how the individual was freed from his bondage by *showing fearlessness*.

Man should watch himself hourly to detect if his motive for action is fear or faith.

"Choose ye this day whom we shall serve," fear or faith.

Perhaps one's fear is of personality. Then do not avoid the people feared; be willing to meet them cheerfully, and they will either prove "golden links in the chain of one's good" or disappear harmoniously from one's pathway.

Perhaps one's fear is of disease or germs. Then one should be fearless and undisturbed in a germ-laden situation, and he would be immune.

One can only contract germs while vibrating at the same rate as the germ, and fear drags men down to the level of the germ. Of course, the disease-laden germ is the product of carnal mind, as all thought must objectify. Germs do not exist in the superconscious or Divine Mind, therefore are the product of man's "vain imagination."

"In the twinkling of an eye," man's release will come when he realizes *there is no power in evil.*

_____

_____

_____

_____

_____

_____

_____

_____

_____

_____

_____

_____

_____

The material world will fade away, and the fourth dimensional world, the "World of the Wondrous," will swing into manifestation.

"And I saw a new heaven, and a new earth — and there shall be no more death, neither sorrow nor crying, neither shall there be any more pain; for the former things are passed away."

WORKBOOK SESSION SIX

Casting the Burden

Topics:

- Casting the Burden
- Burdens Are Fear Energy
- Negativity of Others
- Guidance to Dealing with Negativity
- Casting the Burden for Clear Vision
- Active Faith and Anchoring

- A Powerful Anchoring Tool
- The Energy of "Want"
- Fear
- God Is the Giver and the Receiver
- Recap and Personal Journal

Begin this session by breathing deeply to achieve balance. Surround yourself with God's Divine White Light of Protection and set your intention to connect with your Higher Self.

Father, Mother, God, Creator of All That Is…

I claim my personal power and open the way to see clearly my Field of Potentiality, my field of infinite possibilities. I cut the ties of beliefs and thought patterns that no longer serve me in all directions of time, removing them from my consciousness, my subconscious, and my superconscious. I fearlessly step into the magnificence of the true essence of who I am — One with God. I graciously accept all that is mine by Divine Right, under grace in a miraculous way and commit to fulfill all that I came to be, have, and do in this incarnation on Mother Earth at this time.

Amen

Ask your guides, angels, and teachers to be present with you to help you open your heart, mind, and spirit to the infinite possibilities of you.

CASTING THE BURDEN

In Chapter 6, Casting the Burden, we receive more guidance to identifying resistance and fear within us. Florence states that man violates spiritual law if he carries a burden — our burdens being our worries and fears. He violates the law because he puts his fears and worries — his burdens — above the power of God. To give all our burdens to God requires complete Trust that God can handle them, that He is our supply in all things. In order to completely trust in God, man must release his desire to control.

We worry, we fret, we fear, and we're taught that these burdens are necessary to live a responsible life. The idea of living a responsible life is to be in control. When we feel the need to control, we live from a source of fear — separate from God. If we aren't working with God, then we're working with the physical world and the physical world is fear, worry, limiting ourselves, resentment, lack, and judgment — burdens.

Florence teaches us to be responsible, and trust God to care for us, giving our control to Him to be our supply. Is this responsible behavior?

It is the ONLY responsible behavior.

In order to cast all our burdens aside and live free in the hand of God we must rid ourselves of fearful thought — of physical world conditioning. We must raise our level of consciousness.

And how do we do this? How do we "cast" the fears that become our burdens?

Within the palm of God is safety. We humans seek safety in tapping into the lifeline of God we will be able to release the hold we have on the familiar — fear and doubt. It is very sad that fear and doubt become normal and familiar, like breathing, but it is true. In setting the intention and making our connection with God, we open the door to allow ourselves to feel the love of God, to experience the all-encompassing comfort and safety of the love that we are. It is at this time that our energetic vibration will elevate and we will be able to grasp the concept of life without doubt and fear.

Before experiencing this workbook, had we been asked if we were living in fear source or love source, the majority of us would have responded without thinking, that we were in love source.

27 ▶ INSIDE ASSIGNMENT

Signs of Fear Today we're getting a clear understanding that everything outside of LOVE is fear source. Read through the following list and circle everything that you have experienced this week. Everything in this list is of fear source. Then ask yourself, "why did I experience this?" and write the "why" in the space. Be open to what is revealed to you. Use your tools to face what is revealed to you and shift your energy from less than love to love.

When we are truly in love source, none of the items in the list are present. Now we're seeing the pattern of thought processes that the physical world has taught us as our "Normal state of being" and those thought processes are fear based.

Use the Personal Journal to write about your discoveries in completing this exercise.

Anxiety	Helplessness
Anxiousness	Feeling overwhelmed
Hatred	Stress
Anger	Sadness
Depression	Resistance
Frustration	Angst
Aggravation	Sorrow
Irritation	Worry
Doubt	Concern
Guilt	Nervousness
Shame	Resentment

_____

_____

_____

_____

_____

_____

BURDENS ARE FEAR ENERGY

This chapter of Casting the Burden reveals to us fear at yet an even deeper level. The root of all "burden" is fear. Fear is resistance. We've learned how to identify resistance within us. It's that twinge within our truth center that signals to us that we've docked with an opportunity to heal and raise our vibration. The caution light has come on to look ahead for perfection in what may appear to be a situation of adversity.

Acknowledging perfection in a situation is the first step to shifting us from panic and anguish of helpless resistance to the peaceful tranquility of non-resistance. There is perfection in all situations, whether we see it or not, and that perfection is our golden opportunity to heal within and elevate our energetic vibration.

When we experience a situation and we feel that familiar twinge of resistance, pat yourself on the back because "noticing the pang of resistance" is becoming your New Normal. As you work through the workbook, taking the action steps within to dissolve the resistance will become your New Normal. This resistance within is the burden that Florence speaks of. Let's refer back to the three levels of consciousness.

- Conscious, or reasoning mind, has identified there is resistance within.

- Subconscious is housing the resistance that is being mirrored back to us in the life situation.

- Superconscious is where our power, the Higher Self or Divinity, within us resides. It is from this space that we heal the situation and shift from a resistant to non-resistant state.

It is in the superconscious mind that the transformation occurs. This is where our faith and trust in our connection with God brings us balance, peace, and comfort.

In the Inside Assignment we again visit our Square of Life and assess whether we have resistance in an area. As you work through the workbook you experience transformation and healing deep within and yet more suppressed fear is revealed. At times the revelation may be elusive, so revisiting the Square of Life Form shines the light on all that can be healed at this time.

With each session of this workbook, you tap more deeply into the Life Force Energy of Creation within you. With each session you strip away layer after layer of physical world conditioning and shift more into love source.

28 ▶ INSIDE ASSIGNMENT

More Growth   As you read the sections of the Square of Life Form, review/examine the emotions that are generated by each section. Do this HONESTLY! Do you feel anxious in an area, fearful, joyful, and/or confident? What are the worry burdens hiding behind false confidence? Write down your feelings as you work your way through the form.

SQUARE OF LIFE

HEALTH	WEALTH
A healthy physical body that houses our spirit	Cash flow that fulfills our needs and desires

LOVE	PERFECT SELF-EXPRESSION
Relationships that are fulfilling and love based	Work that fulfills our passion

NEGATIVITY OF OTHERS

Fear is rampant across the planet of Mother Earth. Existing in a core state of fear is how we are taught to live. Each person is dealing with their own "ascension stepping stone" by experiencing firsthand their innermost fears being shoved into their faces by the new energies affecting Mother Earth. Most people don't know why this is happening. This workbook sheds light on how the energy of the planet is affecting us and gives you tools to work through it, heal, and evolve.

You are learning how to flow in ease and grace as Mother Earth evolves to a higher state of existence, however you are human and you are touched by negative energies of others in your community, workplace, and possibly in your home.

When you are able to maintain the love source vibration you initiate healing for yourself, your geographic location *and* as a ripple effect your healing within touches the people around you in a positive way. Others will want to know what you're doing! Those who aren't interested in shifting from fear source to love will fade from your life and/or become a non-issue.

There are some people who are NOT interested in healing within — they are not ready to step into their power and we must honor them in their decision.

The following is a guideline of tools to help you stay in love source while those around you are not.

GUIDELINES TO DEALING WITH NEGATIVITY

1. **Acknowledge** that you are feeling the negativity from others; pat yourself on the back for being in your New Normal State!

2. **Pinpoint the Burden/Resistance** you are feeling within you as a result of coming into contact with the negative energy.

3. **Shift the Resistance/Fear** within you to love source: sincerely send love and blessings from your heart to the negative situation, relationship, or yourself (if you are the source) to transmute your fear energy resistance to love energy. You may use the bonus gift "Shift Your Energy to Love" technique (www.GameOfLifeMastery.com/freegift)

4. **Bless** those who are negative sincerely from the heart.

5. **Recognize** their spiritual essence in a positive light instead of considering their weakness or negativity.

6. **Rethink** your past reactions to negativity and avoid being a victim.

Remember the negative energy that is touching you is mirroring back to you something that is going on within you. When you face this burden/resistance, you will heal it and then the negative situation or person will fade away. Use the next Inside Assignment to get clear on your Energy of Creation — negative/fear or positive/love?

NOTE: you are where you are for a reason. You are an instrument of healing for your geographic location and the humans around you. You are shining the light for those who are seeking. Those who are not interested will fade from the picture. Don't take this on as a task — it simply "IS." As you heal, you send out a ripple effect of healing to everything around you, including Mother Earth.

29 ## INSIDE ASSIGNMENT

Creation Energy Think about something you wanted to be, do, or have prior to and during experiencing this workbook. Write it down in the I Wanted to Be, Do, or Have" column. Then evaluate what happened and write it down in the appropriate column. Through this exercise you will learn how to recognize the Creation Energy of Love and the Creation Energy of Fear.

Use the Personal Journal to write about your experience identifying your turning points — when you chose to have faith and to trust or when you chose to negate receipt with fear and doubt.

FAITH AND TRUST

I Wanted to Be, Do, or Have	Results	Allowed Faith and Trust	Allowed Fear and Doubt

CASTING THE BURDEN FOR CLEAR VISION

Florence states "in casting the burden, after a little while, one seems to see clearly. It is impossible to have clear vision while in the throes of carnal mind. Doubts and fear poison the mind and body and imagination runs riot, attracting disaster and disease." When we "believe" or "focus" on fear-based thoughts, our vision is obscured by the lower vibration of the fear energy.

Florence also states "casting the burden enables one to see in the dark." The "dark" is the illusion of fear that man has created. Much of the physical world is "of the dark" riddled in fear-based teachings. When we "cast the burden" or heal the resistance of fear within us, we see clearly in the darkness of human existence.

As you implement Florence's teachings you are shifting into a clearer vision of who you are and your place here on the planet. However, the vision may not be clear in all the areas of your Square of Life. Know that the process has begun and that the haze obscuring your vision is the fear you have yet to heal.

Again, you may not actively feel as though you are living in fear, but when you know you aren't fully in love source, you are in fear — anything that isn't love is fear. Remember your guidelines of tools to access the resistance within you that holds you hostage, the veil that prevents clear vision. Implement them.

ACTIVE FAITH AND ANCHORING

Active faith is putting our feelings of gratitude within into action for what we have asked for when there is no sign of it in sight. We've discussed this before, but as humans, getting our mind around this can be challenging, because it goes against physical world teachings and conditioning.

Active faith anchors belief of receiving in the Universe. Anchoring it in the Universe writes the record of our subconscious as if we have received — then the subconscious works behind the scenes, manifesting the item or event into our reality.

When we go into a restaurant and place our order, we don't go into the kitchen to make sure the cook or chef prepares what we ordered. Instead we sit at our table preparing to receive our food. Sometimes we can even taste it. This is definitely showing active faith and experiential visualization!

There are unlimited ways to anchor our requests. These are but a few:

- Writing desires in a journal

- Affirming receipt through affirmations

- Visualizing receipt

- Celebrating receipt

A POWERFUL ANCHORING TOOL

We live in an abundant Universe. The Universe does not distinguish whether we want a glass of water because we're thirsty or a new house because we're being evicted from the old one. It simply matches to us that which matches our energy. This is why it is SO important that we discern the energy of what we desire, release any fear surrounding what we want, and request to receive it by Divine Right under grace in a wonderful way.

The Universal Supply Warehouse Order Form in the next Inside Assignment walks you through, step by step, the activation of your Creation Energy to manifest what you want as your reality.

30 ▶ INSIDE ASSIGNMENT

Time to Order This exercise will activate your Creation Energy by placing an order with the Universal Supply Warehouse.

ORDER FORM

1. Get clear on what you want to be, do, or have. Face any "resistance" energy and shift your energetic vibration to the higher vibration of love.

2. Fill in the Universal Supply Warehouse Form

   Description: Describe what you want - embracing the joy filled energy of receipt

   Price: Joy-filled energy of receipt

   Shipping and Handling: Under grace in a wonderful way

   Delivery Date: At the right time

   Place Your Order: Sign and date the form

3. Embrace and maintain the joy-filled energy of receipt as much as possible. Acknowledge guidance of action steps, if there are any, and confidently take them. If doubt slips in, stop what you're doing and identify the core of the fear/doubt energy and neutralize it, shifting back into the higher energy level of the joy of receipt.

4. Visualize receipt in gratitude

5. Receive the desire with gratitude

After completing the assignment, ask yourself: Did you find yourself feeling confident as you filled out the form? Or did you feel skeptical or unworthy? If your order does not resonate with you, look within to discern why. Were your inner and outer voices in alignment? If they are not, look within and discern the resistance and use your tools to bring them into alignment.

Once you have your inner and outer voices in alignment, either make a copy of the form or rewrite the order on a piece of paper that you can keep with you. At least once per day, take out the paper, read through your order, and visualize what it would feel like, taste like, smell like, and be like to receive your order. Repeat this exercise until the Universe fills your order.

You may download a pdf file of the Universal Supply Warehouse form at www.GameOfLifeMastery.com/freegift.

UNIVERSAL SUPPLY WAREHOUSE ORDER FORM

Description of Desire	Price
A new computer	Embrace the joy-filled energy of having received when there is no sign of it in sight.
A relationship based on love and mutual respect	

Shipping and Handling

Under grace in a wonderful way

Delivery Date

At the right time

Ordered by Divine Right by: _____

Date: _____

THE ENERGY OF "WANT"

When we "want" something there is an energy attached to the desire. This energy is either love based or fear based. If the energy associated with the term "want" is fear based, then the fear will block us from manifesting what we desire. We may receive all kinds of signs of paradise coming but never receive it because we don't take the opportunity to heal the fear of our "want." Distinguishing the energy of our "wants" or desires and transmuting the fear energy to love will assure receipt of what we want.

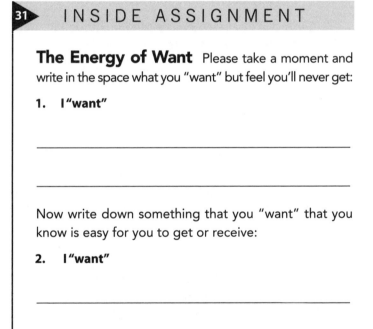

31 ▶ I N S I D E   A S S I G N M E N T

The Energy of Want Please take a moment and write in the space what you "want" but feel you'll never get:

1.   I "want"

_____

_____

Now write down something that you "want" that you know is easy for you to get or receive:

2.   I "want"

_____

_____

Notice the energy associated with each desire as you read them aloud. Use the Personal Journal to explore what you learned in this exercise.

FEAR

Jesus Christ said, "Why are ye fearful, O ye of little faith?" "All things are possible to him that believeth."

Florence states that fear is misdirected energy and must be redirected or transmuted into faith.

Fear in our physical world mind is very real and will eat us alive if we allow it to. It even has the ability to manifest itself into very frightening things through the power that we give it, yet it is still an illusion. However, we have the power to dissipate it from our lives. It is, indeed, a choice.

Florence responded to being asked, "How can I get rid of Fear?" with "By walking up to the thing you are afraid of." The reasoning mind would ask, how will I walk up to what I'm afraid of when most of my fears are not tangible things like fear of failure, fear of success, or fear of being let down — again.

This is when the healing process isn't confronting the person or life situation. The work is within us, not outside of us. We walk up to the thing we are afraid of by discerning the resistance within us. When we discern our burden — where our resistance is — then we can "cast" it away and step firmly into our power and be freed from bondage!

Florence suggests monitoring our motives hourly to determine the basis for what we do. In monitoring ourselves we discern: are our actions fear-based or love-based? Remember there is no in between.

GOD IS THE GIVER AND THE RECEIVER

Let us open our minds to understand God being the giver and the receiver. Each one of us has a Higher Self within, therefore, when we give, in love, to others, we elevate our vibrational frequency and the Universe "matches" high vibrational frequencies of prosperity back to us. As our Higher Self gives to others, our Higher Self also receives the good back from the act of giving.

NOTE: When we give, we will receive something back. If we refuse to accept the gift that is given back to us, we violate spiritual law by intentionally blocking gifts from the Universe. This stops our flow of abundance as well as the person giving to us.

Know that man cannot out-give God. You will find that in giving to others, you will receive prosperity from the Universe, from God. Try to out-give Him and you will experience an avalanche of prosperity!

 INSIDE ASSIGNMENT

Receive by Giving The following activity will share God's love with others, elevate your vibrational frequency, knowing the Universe will "match" back to you what you give out. Doing any of these suggestions will consciously set in motion good, love-based works. You will "seed" good things for yourself and you will be sharing with others blessings you have received — giving from your heart. You will learn you cannot out-give God!

Suggestions:

1. Pay for the meal of the person behind you at a drive-through window.

2. Pay the toll for the vehicle behind you on a toll road.

3. As you are leaving a restaurant, pay for the meal of the table next to you. In paying as you are leaving, you are able to remain anonymous.

4. When checking out at the grocery store, purchase a gift card and give it to someone in line or give it to the manager or clerk to forward to the next person in line — this way you remain anonymous.

5. Contact a local elementary school and donate new underwear, socks, coats, etc., for the children.

6. Contact a local school, homeless shelter, nursing home, or hospital and sponsor a child or family for Christmas.

7. Leave coins in the change dispenser for the next person who comes along.

8. Leave a roll of quarters and/or laundry detergent with a note that it is a gift for the person who discovers it at a laundromat.

9. Volunteer.

Talk about a natural high. Giving to others anonymously is so much fun! Use the Personal Journal to write about your experience and how you felt. Be sure to include the amazing gifts/blessings you receive.

RECAP

Our mission this lifetime in the physical world is to shift our energy from the illusion of fear to the Christ Consciousness of love to create our version of Heaven on Earth as our reality.

This chapter, Casting the Burden, moves us to a level of understanding that leaves awe in the human brain. The tools provided through *The Game of Life Workbook* will aid in achieving Christ Consciousness. Your entourage of angels, guides, and teachers will help you to become immune to the physical world teachings of fear and doubt. Work with your angelic team to maintain a grounding of consciousness. Your life will be easier and the prosperous abundance you desire will be quicker to manifest.

Your spiritual growth is blooming tenfold. Allow it to be. Pray. Ask God to make your life easier. Ask Him to give you the clear eyes to see Him around you. Ask Him to give you clear hearing and knowing to understand His presence and His guidance. Graciously allow yourself to receive these things.

Use the Personal Journal to evaluate what you have learned in this section. Be sure to thank your angelic entourage for being in attendance and helping you to clearly understand God's work.

May you be profoundly blessed in this moment and in every moment after.

PERSONAL JOURNAL

_____

_____

_____

_____

_____

_____

_____

_____

_____

_____

_____

PERSONAL JOURNAL

CHAPTER 7

Love

■ ■ ■ ■ ■

*E*very man on this planet is taking his initiation in love. "A new commandment I give unto you, that ye love one another." Ouspensky states, in "Tertium Organum," that "love is a cosmic phenomenon," and opens to man the fourth dimensional world, "The World of the Wondrous."

Real love is selfless and free from fear. It pours itself out upon the object of its affection, without demanding any return. Its joy is in the joy of giving. Love is God in manifestation, and the strongest magnetic force in the Universe. Pure, unselfish love *draws to itself its own*; it does not need to seek or demand. Scarcely anyone has the faintest conception of real love. Man is selfish, tyrannical, or fearful in his affections, thereby losing the thing he loves. Jealousy is the worst enemy of love, for the imagination runs riot, seeing the loved one attracted to another, and invariably these fears objectify if they are not neutralized.

For example: A woman came to me in deep distress. The man she loved had left her for other women, and said he never intended to marry her. She was torn with jealousy and resentment and said she hoped he would suffer as he had made her suffer, and added, "How could he leave me when I loved him so much?"

I replied, "You are not loving that man, you are hating him," and added, *"You can never receive what you have never given. Give a perfect love and you will receive a perfect love. Perfect yourself on this man. Give him a perfect, unselfish love, demanding nothing in return, do not criticize or condemn, and bless him wherever his is."*

She replied, "No, I won't bless him unless I know where he is!" she said.

"Well," I said, "that is not real love."

"When you *send out real love,* real love will return to you, either from this man or his equivalent, for if this man is not the divine selection, you will not want him. As you are one with God, you are one with the love which belongs to you by Divine Right."

Several months passed, and matters remained about the same, but she was working conscientiously with herself. I said, "When you are no longer disturbed by his cruelty, he will cease to be cruel, as you are attracting it through your own emotions."

Then I told her of a brotherhood in India, who never said, "good morning" to each other. They used these words: *"I salute the Divinity in you."* They saluted the divinity in every man, and in the wild animals in the jungle, and they were never harmed, for they *saw only God in every* living thing. I said, "Salute the divinity in this man, and say, 'I see your Divine Self only. I see you as God sees you, perfect, made in His image and likeness.'"

She found she was becoming more poised, and gradually losing her resentment. He was a Captain, and she always called him "The Cap."

One day, she said, suddenly, *"God bless the Cap wherever he is."*

I replied: "Now that is real love, and when you have become a 'complete circle,' and are no longer disturbed by the situation, you will have his love, or attract its equivalent."

I was moving at this time, and did not have a telephone, so was out of touch with her for a few weeks, when one morning I received a letter saying, "We are married."

At the earliest opportunity, I paid her a call. My first words were, "What happened?"

"Oh," she exclaimed, "a miracle! One day I woke up and all suffering had ceased. I saw him that evening and he asked me to marry him. We were married in about a week, and I have never seen a more devoted man."

There is an old saying: *"No man is your enemy, no man is your friend, every man is your teacher."*

So one should become impersonal and learn what each man has to teach him, and soon he would learn his lessons and be free.

The woman's lover was teaching her selfless love, which every man, sooner or later, must learn.

Suffering is not necessary for man's development; it is the result of violation of spiritual law, but few people seem able to rouse themselves from their "soul sleep" without it. When people are happy, they usually become selfish, and automatically the law of Karma is set in action. Man often suffers loss through lack of appreciation.

I knew a woman who had a very nice husband, but she said often, "I don't care anything about being married, but that is nothing against my husband. I'm simply not interested in married life."

She had other interests, and scarcely remembered she had a husband. She only thought of him when she saw him. One day her husband told her he was in love with another woman, and left. She came to me in distress and resentment.

I replied, "It is exactly what you spoke the word for. You said you didn't care anything about being married, so the subconscious worked to get you unmarried."

She said, "Oh yes, I see. People get what they want, and then feel very much hurt."

She soon became in perfect harmony with the situation, and knew they were both much happier apart.

When a woman becomes indifferent or critical, and ceases to be an inspiration to her husband, he misses the stimulus of their early relationship and is restless and unhappy.

A man came to me dejected, miserable, and poor. His wife was interested in the "Science of Numbers," and had had him read. It seems the report was not very favorable, for he said, "My wife says I'll never amount to anything because I am a two."

I replied, "I don't care what your number is, you are a perfect idea in Divine Mind, and we will demand the success and prosperity which are *already planned* for you by that Infinite Intelligence."

Within a few weeks, he had a very fine position, and a year or two later, he achieved a brilliant success as a writer. No man is a success in business unless he loves his work. The picture the artist paints for love (of his art) is his greatest work. The potboiler is always something to live down.

No man can attract money if he despises it. Many people are kept in poverty by saying: "Money means nothing to me, and I have a contempt for people who have it."

———————————

———————————

———————————

———————————

———————————

———————————

———————————

———————————

———————————

———————————

———————————

———————————

———————————

———————————

This is the reason so many artists are poor. Their contempt for money separates them from it.

I remember hearing one artist say of another, "He's no good as an artist; he has money in the bank."

This attitude of mind, of course, separates man from his supply; he must be in harmony with a thing in order to attract it.

Money is God in manifestation, as freedom from want and limitation, but it must be always kept in circulation and put to right uses. Hoarding and saving react with grim vengeance.

This does not mean that man should not have houses and lots, stocks, and bonds, for "the barns of the righteous man shall be full." It means man should not hoard even the principal, if an occasion arises, when money is necessary. In letting it go out fearlessly and cheerfully he opens the way for more to come in, for God is man's unfailing and inexhaustible supply.

This is the spiritual attitude towards money and the great Bank of the Universal never fails!

We see an example of hoarding in the film production of *Greed*. The woman won five thousand dollars in a lottery, but would not spend it. She hoarded and saved, let her husband suffer and starve, and eventually she scrubbed floors for a living.

She loved the money itself and put it above everything, and one night she was murdered and the money taken from her.

This is an example of where "love of money is the root of all evil." Money in itself is good and beneficial, but used for destructive purposes, hoarded and saved, or considered more important than love, brings disease and disaster, and the loss of the money itself.

Follow the path of love, and all things are added, *for God is love, and God is supply*; follow the path of selfishness and greed, and the supply vanishes, or man is separated from it.

For example: I knew the case of a very rich woman who hoarded her income. She rarely gave anything away, but bought and bought things for herself.

She was very fond of necklaces, and a friend once asked her how many she possessed. She replied, "sixty-seven." She bought them and put them away, carefully wrapped in tissue paper. Had she used the necklaces it would have been quite legitimate, but she was violating "the law of use." Her closets were filled with clothes she never wore, and jewels that never saw the light.

The woman's arms were gradually becoming paralyzed from holding on to things, and eventually she was considered incapable of looking after her affairs and her wealth was handed over to others to manage.

So man, in ignorance of the law, brings about his own destruction.

All disease, all unhappiness, come from the violation of the law of love. Man's boomerangs of hate, resentment, and criticism come back laden with sickness and sorrow. Love seems almost a lost art, but the man with the knowledge of spiritual law knows it must be regained, for without it, he has "become as sounding brass and tinkling cymbals."

For example: I had a student who came to me, month after month, to clean her consciousness of resentment. After a while, she arrived at the point where she resented only one woman, but that one woman kept her busy. Little by little she became poised and harmonious, and one day, all resentment was wiped out.

She came in radiant, and exclaimed "You can't understand how I feel! The woman said something to me and instead of being furious I was loving and kind, and she apologized and was perfectly lovely to me. No one can understand the marvelous lightness I feel within!"

Love and goodwill are invaluable in business.

For example: A woman came to me, complaining of her employer. She said she was cold and critical and knew she did not want her in the position.

"Well," I replied, "salute the Divinity in the woman and send her love."

She said, "I can't; she's a marble woman."

I answered, "You remember the story of the sculptor who asked for a certain piece of marble. He was asked why he wanted it, and he replied, 'because there is an angel in the marble,' and it he produced a wonderful work of art."

She said, "Very well, I'll try it." A week later she came back and said, "I did what you told me to, and now the woman is very kind, and took me out in her car."

People are sometimes filled with remorse for having done someone an unkindness, perhaps years ago.

If the wrong cannot be righted, its effect can be neutralized by doing some one a kindness *in the present.*

"This one thing I do, forgetting those things which are behind and reaching forth unto those things where are before."

_____

_____

_____

_____

_____

_____

_____

_____

_____

_____

_____

_____

_____

_____

_____

Sorrow, regret, and remorse tear down the cells of the body, and poison the atmosphere of the individual.

A woman said to me in deep sorrow, "Treat me to be happy and joyous, for my sorrow makes me so irritable with members of my family that I keep making more Karma."

I was asked to treat a woman who was mourning for her daughter. I denied all belief in loss and separation, and affirmed that God was the woman's joy, love, and peace.

The woman gained her poise at once, but sent word by her son, not to treat any longer, because she was "so happy, it wasn't respectable."

So "mortal mind" loves to hang onto its griefs and regrets.

I knew a woman who went about bragging of her troubles, so, of course, she always had something to brag about.

The old idea was if a woman did not worry about her children, she was not a good mother.

Now we know that mother-fear is responsible for many of the diseases and accidents that come into the lives of children.

For fear pictures vividly the disease or situation feared, and these pictures objectify, if not neutralized.

Happy is the mother who can say sincerely that she puts her child in God's hands, and knows therefore, that he is divinely protected.

For example: A woman awoke suddenly in the night, feeling her brother was in great danger. Instead of giving into her fears, she commenced making statements of Truth, saying, "Man is a perfect idea in Divine Mind, and is always in his right place, therefore, my brother is in his right place, and is divinely protected."

The next day she found that her brother had been in close proximity to an explosion in a mine, but had miraculously escaped.

So man is his brother's keeper (in thought) and every man should know that the thing he loves dwells in "the secret place of the most high, and abides under the shadow of the Almighty."

"There shall no evil befall thee, neither shall any plague come nigh thy dwelling."

"Perfect love casteth out fear. He that feareth is not made perfect in love," and "Love is the fulfilling of the Law."

WORKBOOK SESSION SEVEN

Topics:

- Unconditional Love
- My Enemy Is My Golden Opportunity
- Is Suffering Necessary?
- Divine Right
- Money Is Not a Problem Solver

- Work That You Love
- Allowing Love to Heal
- Love of Self
- Recap and Personal Journal

Begin this session by breathing deeply to achieve balance. Surround yourself with God's Divine White Light of Protection and set your intention to connect with your Higher Self.

Father, Mother, God, Creator of All That Is…

I claim my personal power and open the way to see clearly my Field of Potentiality, my field of infinite possibilities. I cut the ties of beliefs and thought patterns that no longer serve me in all directions of time, removing them from my consciousness, my subconscious, and my superconscious. I fearlessly step into the magnificence of the true essence of who I am — One with God. I graciously accept all that is mine by Divine Right, under grace in a miraculous way and commit to fulfill all that I came to be, have, and do in this incarnation on Mother Earth at this time.

Amen

Ask your guides, angels, and teachers to be present with you to help you open your heart, mind, and spirit to the infinite possibilities of you.

UNCONDITIONAL LOVE

In Chapter 7, titled simply Love, we're introduced to the true essence of whom and what we are: love.

Florence states that "Love is God in manifestation, and the strongest magnetic force in the Universe. Pure, unselfish love draws to itself its own; it does not need to seek or demand."

Our angels tell us our Soul Purpose is to love. The physical world teaches us we are physical beings limited by race, environment, education, geography, sex, and religion, to name a few. Yet we have this longing within us to set aside these teachings and open our hearts to the true divinity within us, to open our hearts to the essence of whom and what we are: love.

The human brain has only physical world teachings to pull from and the physical world teaches that love is painful. We are betrayed when we trust, when we love and we don't receive what we expect. People we love let us down, stomp on our hearts and kick us aside — even our family. And our family is "supposed to love us unconditionally," per physical world teachings.

Man uses the word "love" to express his feelings about lots of things: oranges, the color blue, the Dallas Cowboys, a new car. We love the new partner in our lives. It takes great maturity to love unconditionally, to love unselfishly, to allow love to "be."

After my dad died in 2005, we wrote the book *Waiting in the Other Room* together. As I was typing his portions of the book, he talked about how the love of the spirit world is more than our human brains can take in. The day after my dear friend, Barbara Mark, co-author of *Angelspeake, How to Talk with Your Angels,* died, she came to me and excitedly told me that the process of the spirit leaving the physical body in death is more joyous than she can explain. She said the love there defies physical world explanation. As humans, we simply cannot fathom the "ALL" of the love. Yet when we look within and we dissipate the fear that has held us hostage all our lives, we get glimpses of the feeling of peace that is the foundation of love. For fleeting moments we feel the balance of the "ALL" of love.

God is love.
We are love.
We are One with God.

Grasping the fact of this knowledge changes everything that we've been taught by society, religion, media, etc.

We are One with God is an inherent truth.

The foundation of this knowledge has shown the light on that which was in darkness within us. We've set the intention and are actively removing the shackles of core beliefs that no longer serve us and we are seeing clearly our path in the light of love.

The Game of Life teaches us to look within — to eradicate the behaviors that are negative, to forgive ourselves and others, to reconnect with the Higher Self within and learn to love and honor the spiritual being and physical body that is us. Until we do this, we really aren't capable of unconditional love.

In Chapter 7 Florence addresses our human need to "control" people and life situations with the example of the woman who loved The Cap. In the beginning the woman was in "victim" mindset and wished to control The Cap, while holding to the belief that her thought processes and actions were justified because she "loved" him. The woman had fear-based tunnel vision until she spoke with Florence.

Her "love" was possessive and controlling — fear was in charge. Florence shone light on the situation by explaining to the woman that when she moved out of fear into love source, her love would be returned to her by The Cap or his equivalent.

Through her trust in God to bring to her the love/man who was hers by Divine Right, she transmuted from fear source energy to love. When she reached the stage of no longer being disturbed by the situation, unconditional love was free to flow and the Universe was able to "match" her highest good of true love to her.

God loves all unconditionally. No matter what we do, no matter whom we are. As we allow our minds to take in all the basics of true, pure love we are elevated to a higher spiritual level — we understand more fully the concept of love energy.

My Enemy Is My Golden Opportunity

In this chapter Florence also revisits the concept that "No man is your enemy, no man is your friend, every man is your teacher." We've learned that issues and hiccups with people and life situations reveal resistance and fear within us. We've learned these hiccups and issues are really Golden Opportunities to identify fear energy within us and shift to love energy.

When we are faced with an uncomfortable situation, we must stop, look within and discern what is being mirrored back to us. The uncomfortable feeling is a red flag to notify us there is a "Golden Opportunity Ahead!"

The reality is that the people who annoy and irritate us mirror back to us what we don't like about ourselves. The irritation/annoyance we feel within us is our Golden Opportunity to change by healing what we don't like about ourselves and become more balanced in the higher vibration of love energy.

Facing our fears in this way is non-threatening. We are in a safe place working with our angels and guides to help us release the pain of this and past lifetimes. Remind yourself this is a safe place and it is safe to be honest with yourself. Look within to discern the core of the resistance, and then ask for guidance on how best to dissolve the resistance and neutralize the situation.

The next Inside Assignment is a Golden Opportunity to waken your mind to how the people/situations you experience friction with, those who annoy/irritate and push your buttons to get under your skin, are really blessed teachers. People who irritate you are actually mirroring back to you things you do not like about yourself.

33 ▶ I N S I D E A S S I G N M E N T

Golden Opportunity   Sit quietly and think about a person that causes discomfort in your life. Feel the discord and resistance in your body? Write their name and describe what it is about them that irritates and annoys you. Then follow through with the next steps.

Name of person and what irritates and annoys you.

_____

_____

_____

_____

_____

Ask your angels to show you what the person is mirroring to you about yourself that you do not like. Allow yourself to take in whatever comes to you.

_____

_____

_____

_____

_____

Send sincere love of your heart to the person to shift your energy from fear to love and take your power back. You may use the bonus gift "Shift Your Energy to Love" technique (www.GameOfLifeMastery.com/freegift). Write about your experience here.

_____

_____

_____

_____

Remember, change begins within you. You are doing the breathing for your body and you are the only one who can heal the pain and fear of your heart in order to step into your power as a Powerful Master Creator.

When you experience the transformation of fear based feelings of irritation and annoyance to love you will not only heal the relationship with others but will heal the issues within yourself.

Use the Personal Journal to anchor your experience.

IS SUFFERING NECESSARY?

Florence states, "suffering is not necessary for man's development; it is the result of violation of spiritual law." The physical world teaches us that we must suffer to have prosperity in our lives. We're taught through many organized religions that God is punishing and judgmental — feelings of unworthiness often stem from this teaching.

Plus, when we believe we must suffer during our lifetime in the physical world we write "Suffering" as a record in our subconscious. The subconscious then works diligently to manifest suffering in our lives. This record must be rewritten!

The reality is that God loves us unconditionally and we live in an abundant Universe of prosperity where we have a magnificent, limitless Field of Potentiality — our "Kingdom." The Universe does not differentiate between our desire for a tissue or a drink of water or a new house or a new car. We've learned that the Universe doesn't distinguish between what is good for us and what is not good for us; it merely matches vibration to vibration.

 INSIDE ASSIGNMENT

Tools for Joy   Sit quietly and review the tools and Universal Laws you have learned and the changes you have implemented in your life. Now think back about your life before *The Game of Life Workbook*. Think about a limiting thought pattern, belief, attitude, or habit that you practiced that brought you suffering. Write it in the Before/Suffering column. In the After/Joy column, write down the tools you used to identify the behavior, what you did to correct it, and the aftereffects of the change. You may have made these changes consciously or subconsciously.

As you identify your fear-based suffering stage and compare it to your new love-based joy state, even more things you can change may be revealed to you.

Use the Personal Journal to write about your discoveries. Are you seeing that you are using your tools more easily now? Are you recognizing negative behavior more quickly and taking the appropriate steps to change it? Is there a part of your Square of Life that is easier to maintain positive thought patterns and behaviors? Are you using your journal and tools to delve deeper into the parts of your Square of Life that still have negative issues?

This journal section is a profoundly powerful tool. As you look back at your progress you will continue to see this. Be wise — use it — don't skip it — JOURNAL!

SPIRITUAL DEVELOPMENT — SUFFERING VERSUS JOY

Before/Suffering	After/Joy
Limiting thought pattern, belief, attitude, or habit that caused suffering.	Tools used to identify, correct, and alter behavior that produced joy.

DIVINE RIGHT

How do we know if something is in our Field of Potentiality? How do we know it is ours by Divine Right? If we are questioning if something is truly ours, then there is some resistance involved. This resistance may be feelings of unworthiness.

 35 INSIDE ASSIGNMENT

Mine by Divine Right Think of your favorite color and write it in the space:

My favorite color is:

_____

Reflect on this information. When you think of your favorite color, there is no anxiousness, no fear, no guessing, no doubt. When you think of your favorite color it feels good. You like this color, no question.

Now let's look at something you desire that gives you pause. Write in the space after "Is this mine by Divine Right?" something that you would like to have, be, or do, but you aren't sure if it is truly yours.

Is this mine by Divine Right?

_____

_____

The key to discerning if something is truly yours by Divine Right is to recognize if there is resistance attached to it. Go back and reflect on the feeling within you when you think of your favorite color — no anxiousness or doubt. Then think of the desire you wrote down that you're not sure of. Notice the difference in the feeling within you?

Use the tools you've learned to dissipate resistance. If you're able to dissolve the resistance, then it is safe to say it is in your Field of Potentiality; therefore it is yours by Divine Right. Now write an affirmation reflecting this:

I open the way to receive _____

_____

or its equivalent, what is mine by Divine Right, to come to me now under grace in a miraculous way.

Read through your affirmation, does it resonate? Are your inner and outer voices in alignment? Do you feel at peace within? If so, then allow yourself to be open to any action steps you are guided to take or do in order to manifest your desire into your reality.

Being willing to receive the equivalent opens the way for your heart to reveal to you if this is something you truly desire, if your inner and outer voices are in alignment, and if you trust the Universe to deliver your desire to you. It releases your need to control and allows you to release how the Universe may deliver your request.

If you still feel resistance, sit quietly and look within to discern the source. You may find that what you thought you desired is not what you really want at all, in which case you will know that it is NOT in your Field of Potentiality and you are then able to focus your attention on what you truly desire. Use the Personal Journal to reflect on what you've learned about yourself.

MONEY IS NOT A PROBLEM SOLVER

We understand from Chapter 2 that money will not solve our problems. We use our thoughts, beliefs, and words to block receipt of abundance. Florence shares with us the example of an artist whose contempt of money blocked his attracting money to him. His contempt for money wrote in his subconscious record that money was bad, so the artist did not receive money.

Florence states that "Money is God in manifestation, as freedom from want and limitation, but it must be kept in circulation and put to right uses. Hoarding and saving react with grim vengeance."

Let's take a moment and get our minds around, "Money is God in manifestation, as freedom from want and limitation." This tells us that to become one with God does not mean that we will live our lives in lack and limitation. It means that money *is* simply energy — a form of supply.

Money IS energy. What kind of energy are we giving it? When we "want" more money, are we giving it "fear based don't have enough want energy" or "love based joy of having want energy?" Is there resistance surrounding it or do we feel the flow of ease and grace?

In the Chapter 6 workbook session we discussed the energy of "Want." When we use the term "want" while we are in fear source, then the want energy is of the lower vibration of fear and we will attract more of "don't have enough" want energy.

When we use the term "want" while we are in love source — without fear — then the "want energy" is of the higher vibration of love and we will draw to us (the Universe will match to us) what we desire.

Dissolving our fear where money is concerned opens the channels for the Universe to shower us with avalanches of prosperous abundance and that may very well be in the form of cash flow.

Money is a part of our source of providing material things, so money is also in our Field of Potentiality as proved with Florence "speaking the word and treating" for people to receive money. When we hold money in the energy of love we will receive it in miraculous ways.

 INSIDE ASSIGNMENT

Money Without Limits Look within and discern your thoughts, feelings, and beliefs about money. Use the Personal Journal to write about your experience with money. Are you afraid to let it go? Do you pay bills with gratitude as if you have a limitless supply — more than you can spend? Or do you pay bills riddled with fear?

WORK THAT YOU LOVE

Many of us choose our work without consulting what we love to do. We fail to look within to find the spark that ignites our flame of creativity. In the "perfect idea of Divine Mind," there is a fulfilling service for each of us. It may not be what our families or friends want us to do or even our logical, physical world "reasoning mind." However, in Divine Mind, there is an important place for us to share our talents and gifts with the world. Finding this work is true success — the rewards are fulfilled love and a deep joy within at the ability to bring the service to the world.

Florence states that "No man is a success in business unless he loves his work." The physical world associates "success" with money and fame. The fact is that true success is the fulfillment of experiencing love. So the full statement would be, "Nobody is a success in life unless they love what they're doing."

We get caught up in the physical world "to do" list and put ourselves last on the list or not at all. Some people love their work or jobs, but many don't. Some hate their work or job. What is the difference between those who don't like their jobs and those who love them? Nothing. Not a thing.

If you don't like your work, ponder your situation. Why are you doing what you're doing? What physical world teaching have you convinced yourself of that you can't change jobs?

Use Florence's teachings and all the other tools you have to discern what would bring you the most joy. Ask and allow God to show you the action steps to take to move you into work that makes your heart sing!

37 INSIDE ASSIGNMENT

Sing Out Loud Use the space below to write about what makes your heart "sing."

_____

_____

_____

_____

_____

_____

_____

_____

What do your inner and outer voices say about this exercise? Do you feel resistance or possibility? What can you do to shift from fear/resistance to love/possibility? Use the Personal Journal to write about your discoveries.

ALLOWING LOVE TO HEAL

We've learned how fear blocks the love of God from helping us — from bringing prosperity to us. It also blocks receipt of healing.

We must hold fast to our trust and faith in God as our supply. Whether it's disease, resentment, grief, or worry, fearing for ourselves and loved ones blocks the flow of love from God, which also blocks the receipt of healing.

Fear does nothing to enhance our lives.

Transmuting fear and worry to a love base doesn't mean we don't care. On the contrary, it proves our faith and trust in God. When we release fear regarding another individual, we open the way for us and the individual to step more fully into personal power.

When we worry about our children, we see them in the darkness of fear. If they are in fear source, more to be fearful of is attracted to them. When we hold our children in the light of powerful master creators, they feel that support of love and light and if they are in fear source, it helps them to crawl out of it into a higher vibration of love. If they are already in the higher vibration of love, yet more doors are opened to them at a higher level of understanding.

Use the Personal Journal to write about your love experience. Are you able to shift out of fear and into peace and an inner joy when you think about your loved one?

LOVE OF SELF

You can only receive as much love from others as you love yourself. Being able to look into a mirror into your own eyes and love yourself from your heart is very important to achieve the change you seek.

 INSIDE ASSIGNMENT

Remnants of Fear This exercise will reveal to you remnants of fear as resistance that still hide within you. Look into your eyes in a mirror. Do not be critical of yourself, no looking for wrinkles or judging yourself. Just look at yourself and say, "I love you."

As you say this to yourself, what do you feel inside? Do you feel love pouring from your heart to yourself? Do you feel silly? Anxious? Fearful? Do you feel love or resistance?

If you feel love pouring from your heart to yourself, then just sit back and relax. If you feel any form of resistance, then assess what the resistance is about. What are you afraid of? Are there any feelings of not good enough?

Use the Personal Journal to record your experience of transformation.

RECAP

This chapter, Love, details bringing love into the physical world. Achieving a state of unconditional love will change your life. Collectively achieving a state of unconditional love will change the world.

We've learned more about our divine life path and are feeling the divine guidance to walk it. The abundance blocks that were ingrained in us before are becoming easier to recognize and dismantle.

Maintaining a positive focus and deflecting negativity has become much easier.

Your level of spiritual enlightenment has blossomed as the days have passed. Do not become discouraged if parts of the workbook are confusing. Simply move on and when you have time, go back to anything you didn't quite grasp earlier. As you move through the book and workbook, items that were once confusing will become clearer.

When you heal from within, you are able to tap into and exist in love energy — without fear. Remember there is no place for fear in love.

Living in love source causes your light to glow brightly, drawing to you those who seek the light. Set boundaries for outside energies. Work with your guides and angels to hold you safe in love source. Remember you are human. Even though you are a limitless spiritual being, you reside in a physical body, a body that is affected by lower energies.

Lower energies will drain your love light and drag you back into the abyss of fear that you've just crawled out of. Work with your guides and angels to set boundaries to help you maintain your light.

Continue to journal — daily if you possibly can. Your journal is a direct gateway to connecting with God and maintaining balance of your three levels of consciousness. It always will be. Daily journaling will bring forward more and more information, more understanding, and more spiritual growth.

When you have a moment, go back through the workbook and identify any areas that may be weak. Review your journal for insights. Use the tools you have learned to transmute the weakness.

May you be profoundly blessed in this moment and in every moment after.

PERSONAL JOURNAL

PERSONAL JOURNAL

CHAPTER 8

Intuition and Guidance

■ ■ ■ ■ ■

There is nothing too great an accomplishment for the man who knows the power of his word, and who follows his intuitive leads. By the word he starts in action unseen forces and can rebuild his body or remold his affairs.

It is, therefore, of the utmost importance, to choose the right words, and the student carefully selects the affirmation he wishes to catapult into the invisible.

He knows that God is his supply, that there is a supply for every demand, and that his spoken word releases this supply.

"Ask and ye shall receive."

Man must make the first move. "Draw nigh to God and He will draw nigh to you."

I have often been asked just how to make a demonstration.

I reply: "Speak the word and then do not do anything until you get a definite lead." Demand the lead, saying, "Infinite spirit, reveal to me the way, let me know if there is anything for me to do."

The answer will come through intuition (or hunch): a chance remark from someone, or a passage in a book, etc., etc. The answers are sometimes quite startling in their exactness. For example: A woman desired a large sum of money. She spoke the words: "Infinite Spirit, open the way for my immediate supply, let all that is mine by Divine Right now reach me, in great avalanches of abundance." Then she added: "Give me a definite lead, let me know if there is anything for me to do."

———————————

———————————

———————————

———————————

———————————

———————————

———————————

———————————

———————————

———————————

———————————

———————————

———————————

———————————

The thought came quickly, "Give a certain friend" (who had helped her spiritually) "a hundred dollars." She told her friend, who said, "Wait and get another lead, before giving it." So she waited, and that day met a woman who said to her, "I gave someone a dollar today; it was just as much for me as it would be for you to give someone a hundred."

This was indeed an unmistakable lead, so she knew she was right in giving the hundred dollars. It was a gift that proved a great investment, for shortly after that, a large sum of money came to her in a remarkable way.

Giving opens the way for receiving. In order to create activity in finances, one should give. Tithing or giving one-tenth of one's income is an old Jewish custom, and is sure to bring increase. Many of the richest men in this country have been tithers, and I have never known it to fail as an investment.

The tenth-part goes forth and returns blessed and multiplied. But the gift or tithe must be given with love and cheerfulness, for "God loveth a cheerful giver." Bills should be paid cheerfully, all money should be sent forth fearlessly and with a blessing.

This attitude of mind makes man master of money. It is his to obey, and his spoken word then opens vast reservoirs of wealth.

Man, himself, limits his supply by his limited vision. Sometimes the student has a great realization of wealth, but is afraid to act.

The vision and action must go hand in hand, as in the case of the man who bought the fur-lined overcoat.

A woman came to me asking me to "speak the word" for a position. So I demanded: "Infinite Spirit, open the way for this woman's right position." Never ask for just "a position," ask for the right position, the place already planned in Divine Mind, as it is the only one that will give satisfaction.

I then gave thanks that she had already received, and that it would manifest quickly. Very soon, she had three positions offered her, two in New York and one in Palm Beach, and she did not know which to choose. I said, "Ask for a definite lead."

The time was almost up and was still undecided, when one day, she telephoned, "When I woke up this morning, I could smell Palm Beach." She had been there before and knew its balmy fragrance.

I replied: "Well, if you can smell Palm Beach from here, it is certainly your lead." She accepted the position, and it proved a great success. Often one's lead comes at an unexpected time.

One day, I was walking down the street, when I suddenly felt a strong urge to go to a certain bakery, a block or two away.

The reasoning mind resisted, arguing, "There is nothing there that you want."

However, I had learned not to reason, so I went to the bakery, looked at everything, and there was certainly nothing there that I wanted, but coming out I encountered a woman I had thought of often, and who was in great need of the help that I could give her.

So often, one goes for one thing and finds another.

Intuition is a spiritual faculty and does not explain, but simply *points the way*.

A person often receives a lead during a "treatment." The idea that comes may seem quite irrelevant, but some of God's leadings are "mysterious."

In the class, one day, I was treating that each individual would receive a definite lead. A woman came to me afterwards, and said: "While you were treating, I got the hunch to take my furniture out of storage and get an apartment." The woman had come to be treated for health. I told her I knew in getting a home of her own, her health would improve, and I added, "I believe your trouble, which is a congestion, has come from having things stored away. Congestion of things causes congestion in the body. You have violated the law of use, and your body is paying the penalty."

So I gave thanks that "*Divine order was established in her mind, body, and affairs.*"

People little dream of how their affairs react on the body. There is a mental correspondence for every disease. A person might receive instantaneous healing through the realization of his body being a perfect idea in Divine Mind, and, therefore, whole and perfect, but if he continues his destructive thinking, hoarding, hating, fearing, condemning, the disease will return.

Jesus Christ knew that all sickness came from sin, but admonished the leper after the healing, to go and sin no more, lest a worse thing come upon him.

So man's soul (or subconscious mind) must be washed whiter than snow for permanent healing; and the metaphysician is always delving deep for the "correspondence."

Jesus Christ said, "Condemn not lest ye also be condemned."

"Judge not, lest ye be judged."

Many people have attracted disease and unhappiness through condemnation of others.

What man condemns in others, he attracts to himself.

For example: A friend came to me in anger and distress, because her husband had deserted her for another woman. She condemned the other woman, and said continually, "She knew he was a married man, and had no right to accept his attentions."

I replied: "Stop condemning the woman, bless her, and be through with the situation, otherwise, you are attracting the same thing to yourself."

She was deaf to my words, and a year or two later, became deeply interested in a married man, herself.

Man picks up a live wire whenever he criticizes or condemns, and may expect a shock.

Indecision is a stumbling block in many a pathway. In order to overcome it, make the statement repeatedly, "*I am always under direct inspiration; I make right decisions, quickly.*"

These words impress the subconscious, and soon one finds himself awake and alert, making his right moves without hesitation. I have found it destructive to look to the psychic plane for guidance, as it is the plane of many minds and not "The One Mind."

As man opens his mind to subjectivity, he becomes a target for destructive forces. The psychic plane is the result of man's mortal thought, and is on the "plane of opposites." He may receive either good or bad messages.

The science of numbers and the reading of horoscopes keep man down on the mental (or mortal) plane, for they deal only with the Karmic path.

I know of a man who should have been dead, years ago, according to his horoscope, but he is alive and a leader of one of the biggest movements in this country for the uplift of humanity.

It takes a very strong mind to neutralize a prophecy of evil. The student should declare, "Every false prophecy shall come to naught; every plan my Father in heaven has not planned shall be dissolved and dissipated, the divine idea now comes to pass."

However, if any good message has ever been given one, of coming happiness, or wealth, harbor and expect it, and it will manifest sooner or later, through the law of expectancy.

Man's will should be used to back the universal will. "I will that the will of God be done."

It is God's will to give every man every righteous desire of his heart, and man's will should be used to hold the perfect vision, without wavering.

The prodigal son said: "I will arise and go to my Father."

It is indeed often an effort of the will to leave the husks and swine of mortal thinking. It is so much easier, for the average person, to have fear than faith; *so faith is an effort of the will.*

As man becomes spiritually awakened he recognizes that any external inharmony is the correspondence of mental inharmony. If he stumbles or falls, he may know he is stumbling or falling in consciousness.

One day, a student was walking along the street condemning someone in her thoughts. She was saying mentally, "That woman is the most disagreeable woman on earth," when suddenly three boy scouts rushed around the corner and almost knocked her over. She did not condemn the boy scouts, but immediately called on the law of forgiveness, and "saluted the divinity" in the woman. Wisdom's way are ways of pleasantness and all her paths are peace.

When one has made his demands upon the Universal, he must be ready for surprises. Everything may seem to be going wrong, when in reality, it is going right.

For example: A woman was told that there was no loss in Divine Mind, therefore, she could not lose anything that belonged to her; anything lost, would be returned, or she would receive its equivalent.

Several years previously, she had lost two thousand dollars. She had loaned the money to a relative during her lifetime, but the relative had died, leaving no mention of it in her will. The woman was resentful and angry, and as she had no written statement of the transaction, she never received the money, so she determined to deny the loss and collect the two thousand dollars from the Bank of the Universal. She had to begin by forgiving the woman, as resentment and unforgiveness close the doors of this wonderful bank.

She made this statement, "I deny loss, there is no loss in Divine Mind, therefore, I cannot lose the two thousand dollars, which belong to me by Divine Right. *"As one door shuts another door opens."*

She was living in an apartment house that was for sale; and in the lease was a clause, stating that if the house was sold, the tenants would be required to move out within ninety days.

Suddenly, the landlord broke the leases and raised the rent. Again, injustice was on her pathway, but this time she was undisturbed. She blessed the landlord, and said, "As the rent has been raised, it means that I'll be that much richer, for God is my supply."

New leases were made out for the advanced rent, but by some divine mistake, the ninety days clause had been forgotten. Soon after, the landlord had an opportunity to sell the house. On account of the mistake in the new leases, the tenants held possession for another year.

The agent offered each tenant two hundred dollars to vacate. Several families moved; three remained, including the woman. A month or two passed, and the agent again appeared. This time he said to the woman, "Will you break your lease for the sum of fifteen hundred dollars?" It flashed upon her, "Here comes the two thousand dollars." She remembered having said to friends in the house, "We will all act together if anything more is said about leaving." So her *lead* was to consult her friends.

These friends said, "Well, if they have offered you fifteen hundred they will certainly give two thousand." So she received a check for two thousand dollars for giving up the apartment. It was certainly a remarkable working of the law, and the apparent injustice was merely opening the way for her demonstration.

It proved that there is no loss, and when man takes his spiritual stand, he collects all that is his from this great Reservoir of Good.

"I will restore to you the years the locusts have eaten."

The locusts are the doubts, fears, resentments, and regrets of mortal thinking.

These adverse thoughts, alone, rob man; for "No man gives to himself but himself, and no man takes away from himself, but himself."

Man is here to prove God and "to bear witness to the truth," and he can only prove God by bringing plenty out of lack, and justice out of injustice.

"Prove me now herewith, saith the Lord of hosts, if I will not open you the windows of heaven, and pour out a blessing, that there shall not be room enough to receive it."

WORKBOOK SESSION EIGHT

Intuition and Guidance

Topics:

- How to Make a Demonstration

- Giving Cheerfully

- Open the Doors of Abundance

- External Inharmony

- Recap and Personal Journal

Begin this session by breathing deeply to achieve balance. Surround yourself with God's Divine White Light of Protection and set your intention to connect with your Higher Self.

Father, Mother, God, Creator of All That Is…

I claim my personal power and open the way to see clearly my Field of Potentiality, my field of infinite possibilities. I cut the ties of beliefs and thought patterns that no longer serve me in all directions of time, removing them from my consciousness, my subconscious, and my superconscious. I fearlessly step into the magnificence of the true essence of who I am — One with God. I graciously accept all that is mine by Divine Right, under grace in a miraculous way and commit to fulfill all that I came to be, have, and do in this incarnation on Mother Earth at this time.

Amen

Ask your guides, angels, and teachers to be present with you to help you open your heart, mind, and spirit to the infinite possibilities of you.

How to Make a Demonstration

Florence was often asked how to make a demonstration, which in twenty-first century terms would be "What action steps do I take to manifest what I desire?" All the workbook sessions for Chapter 8 provide this guidance.

When there is something we desire that we do not have, there is fear blocking us from receiving it. We know this because we've learned that if we can dream of something, it is already ours in our Field of Potentiality.

In discerning what we wish to be, do, or have, we've learned to identify "resistance" (our burden), which is our fear that is our block. In identifying the resistance within us we are then able to dissolve the fear, opening the way for the Universe to match to us what we desire.

To manifest our desire in the quickest way possible, we want to anchor our receipt in the Universe with a "demonstration." In past chapters we read about a lady demonstrating that an apartment was hers by purchasing blankets. Another woman demonstrated she would receive Christmas presents to give by buying wrapping paper. Both these ladies were following their intuition to make their demonstration.

In the first Inside Assignment of this section we learn how to tap into our intuition and discern its validity. Our intuition is that connection with our Higher Self that has full knowledge of what is of our highest good. Florence refers to the guidance of our intuition as a "definite lead" when manifesting our desires.

In Chapter 8, Intuition and Guidance, we're given more tools to bring into alignment our conscious, subconscious, and superconscious minds.

Florence begins with bringing into alignment our understanding of love source. When we're truly in the moment in love source we experience a point in time without fear. We are one with our Field of Potentiality. There are no blocks between us and all that we desire.

The Bible tells us, "Ask and ye shall receive." Florence uses the word "demand."

Previously the energy of "wanting" being of love source or of fear source was addressed. In this chapter Florence sheds light on the energy of "asking." The energy of "asking" is the same as the energy of "wanting" — it may be of fear source or of love source. It is up to us to discern its basis.

When we discern what we truly desire and claim it as ours to the Universe/God (demand, as Florence states) our energy is of confident love source and the act puts into action our desire — we anchor our intent.

To break it down:

1. Discern what we truly desire.

2. "Set the intent" by "claiming our desire formally as ours." Demand or command of the Universal Supply Warehouse/God

Through discernment we set into motion the "unseen forces that can rebuild (man's) body or remold his affairs." By claiming/demanding what we want as ours, we've eradicated fear-based thought patterns and beliefs; we've claimed it, thereby, executing a state of receipt. Demanding /claiming writes the record in our subconscious and solidifies the belief that the object of our desire is already ours.

Note: Know that our thought processes are heavily conditioned by the physical world. As a result our brain typically will begin to think, "I'll never be able to do this, or have this, or receive this," thereby negating our claim for what we desire. Receiving abundance is our birthright — we are the children of God of All That Is. It is up to us as to whether we allow this negative, fear-based thinking to be our focus or not.

The action of claiming our desire anchors in our thought patterns the belief that what we desire is already ours. As a result of maintaining a love-based in-gratitude perspective, there are no worries, no doubts, and no anxieties of "how are we going to receive?" The object of your desire is already yours in Divine Mind. In shifting your energy to confident love source and demanding what you desire, manifestation becomes a detail for the Universe to work out.

Now is the time to demand "a lead" as Florence terms it. Look within and ask the question: What can I do to bring this desire to fruition?

If we desire better health, we may be guided to research nutrition and exercise programs that fit our needs. If it is a relationship, we may be guided to focus on the positive things in the relationship and forgive the things that are negative. If it is a job, we may be guided to research classifieds,

the internet, or put out feelers. If it is financial, we may be guided to look into how to invest large sums of money — even when we don't have two nickels to rub together. These actions continue to anchor in the Universe receipt of our desire.

When we set the intention to align ourselves with recognizing and following the guidance of our intuition, discerning which is our ego human brain and which is our inner light of intuition can be challenging at first. Once we begin distinguishing between the two we can clearly see the darkness of the fear-based ego and the lightness of the love-based intuition.

In learning to recognize and follow the guidance of our intuition, we not only claim our power, but we become miraculous manifestors of what we desire.

While following our "lead" or taking the actions we are guided to take, it is important to maintain the higher vibration of love-based gratitude energy. Gratitude keeps us in love energy. There is no room for fear/doubt in gratitude. Completing our action steps with an attitude of gratitude completely frees the Universe to provide our desire to us in its miraculous way in its miraculous time.

INSIDE ASSIGNMENT

Demonstration You've learned how to: Discern what you truly desire; Set the intention of receiving by claiming formally or demanding your desire; Keep an attitude of gratitude; Implement action of receipt. This exercise is designed to employ these skills in a practical form and put them to work.

1. Sit quietly and think about what you would like to receive or an experience that you would like to have. GET CLEAR on what it is.

2. Set the INTENTION of receiving the desire by CLAIMING/DEMANDING it formerly from God/the Universal Supply Warehouse. (You may use a copy of the previous Universal Supply Warehouse Form.)

3. Imagine how good it feels to enjoy what you wish to Be, Do, and Have. Write in the space the VISUALIZATION of the experience of receipt and the feeling of GRATITUDE ENERGY.

4. Ask God/the Universe for a "lead" or ACTION STEPS that will bring your desire into your reality. Prepare for receipt. Write down your guidance if there is any.

5. As you go about the routine of your day, think about your desire and MAINTAIN YOUR ATTITUDE OF GRATITUDE ENERGY of receipt. The Universe will match your vibrational frequency in its time. Write here about your results.

NOTE: Do NOT ask for money — ask for the item you would purchase with the money. Is there anything else you would like to anchor about this experience? Use the Personal Journal space.

Get Clear
Intention/Claiming/Demanding
Visualization/Gratitude Energy
Action Steps
Maintain Your Attitude of Gratitude Energy

GIVING CHEERFULLY

Florence states, "giving opens the way for receiving. In order to create activity in finances, one should give." In times of financial distress the idea of "giving away money" is enough to send the physical part of us into a panic attack.

The reality is that giving money away without fear, as if you have more than you'll ever need, sends out a signal to the Universe that you have all the money you'll ever need and the Universe matches that frequency of vibration by "matching" to you more money.

This is how the Universal Law of Attraction works. **Always.**

Important Note: If money is given away in fear, the action is fear based and will attract more fear. Identify your source of emotion before giving money away. Make sure it is love based!

Giving cheerfully with love to others opens the door to receipt of same — joy, love, abundance, and prosperity in what you freely, cheerfully, lovingly share. In giving with these emotions, your vibrational frequency is raised; the Universe in turn matches to you that vibrational frequency of people, health, love, and perfect self expression — the Square of Life.

Tithing is typically thought of as ten percent of one's income. Tithing may be given in many ways. A few examples are: cash, time, and/or volunteering.

Florence tells us that bills should be paid cheerfully. Typically the physical world conditioning of money makes paying bills a painful experience. Transmute this pain to gratitude by being thankful for the wonderful roof overhead provided by the mortgage or rent. Transmute the pain of the utility bill by being thankful for the warmth in winter and the cool in summer. Transmute the pain to gratitude and joy. It can be done — it is all in how we perceive the process.

REMEMBER: As we learned in Chapter 6, we cannot out-give God!

40 ▶ INSIDE ASSIGNMENT

The Joy of Tithing This exercise is designed to stir your creativity in tithing. Tithing is an important part of creating cash flow, yet it can be the cause of great anxiety. If tithing creates anxiety, it isn't based in love and you should not do it. The key is to base tithing in love and be a cheerful giver.

In the space provided, list five ways you can tithe that will bring you great joy.

1. _____

2. _____

3. _____

4. _____

5. _____

Implement at least one way of tithing from the list this week. As you practice the act of tithing, you'll discover which way brings you the most joy. Be sure to thank God/The Universe for things that you receive unexpectedly. It is imperative that you allow yourself to receive graciously what the Universe/God sends to you. Do NOT block the universal flow of supply by refusing to receive!

OPEN THE DOORS OF ABUNDANCE

Daily we are subjected to negativity, hatred, unforgiveness, and fear! This happens through radio, TV, road rage/traffic, co-workers, family members, etc. It is up to us to transmute the negativity to love.

We've learned that all our thoughts, emotions, and feelings are either based in love or based in fear — there is no in between.

We've also learned that what we continually focus on we will attract to us. We are creating our future in every moment of our life. What we continually focus on WILL manifest into our lives as our reality.

We can look back at our lives and see how our negative feelings and thought patterns drew to us still more lack, fear, painful relationships and situations, illness, horrible employers or co-workers or friends or even family.

We have successfully created the current life we are living. The question is, "Is this the life we truly desire?"

The prosperity of our Square of Life (Health, Wealth, Love, and Perfect Self-Expression) is directly related to our ability to live from a source of love. Fear-based thought patterns and beliefs are not the key and will not open the door. Love-based thought patterns and beliefs ARE the key!

Universal laws are continually at work in our lives whether we want to acknowledge it or not. Fussing about how things turned out is not going to change anything. Conditions are changed by transmuting negative, fear-based thought patterns and beliefs to love-based thought patterns and beliefs.

When we change within, our reality changes — miraculously, doors to the prosperity we desire open.

 INSIDE ASSIGNMENT

Open the Doors This exercise is designed to help you determine if your Doors of Abundance are open or closed. Is the source of your focus love or fear? Please read each question and answer them honestly.

What were my feelings when I woke this morning? Happy? Sad? Anxious?

_____

_____

As I moved through the first half of my day, how did I allow the physical world to affect me, if at all? (Example: Traffic was a mess and I was worried about being late.)

_____

_____

Evaluate the second half of the day. Was it a loving positive experience or was it fear based, producing anxiety?

_____

_____

Was there a point during the day when I recognized fear-based thoughts and transmuted them to love?

_____

_____

EXTERNAL INHARMONY

This chapter also delves more deeply into internal (or mental) inharmony, reflecting externally as inharmony. Florence gives the example of the woman who was nearly run over as she was condemning someone in her thoughts. This case in point illustrates the creation of inharmony immediately.

Florence states, "As man becomes spiritually awakened he recognizes that any external inharmony is the correspondence of the mental inharmony."

We've learned that when we shift energy within, the energy outside of us is also shifted. This goes both ways, if we shift our energy into fear, situations of fear source manifest into our lives. If we shift our energy into love source, situations of love source manifest into our lives.

INSIDE ASSIGNMENT

External Is Internal The external conditions of your life will reflect what is going on inside of you. Are you living the life you desire? Update your Square of Life and review your life. Are you in harmony in each area of your Square of Life? If not, look within. What is the root of the inharmony? By shifting to a harmonious state of love internally and externally, you will attract what you truly desire.

Through all the work you've invested into shifting your energy from fear to love, you've changed your life path to one of love and light. When you stumble back into fear, don't beat yourself up, simply acknowledge you are in fear, use your tools, and shift your energy back into love source.

Use the Personal Journal to write about your experience in shifting your internal affairs to reflect the life you wish to live externally.

SQUARE OF LIFE

HEALTH	**WEALTH**
A healthy physical body that houses our spirit	Cash flow that fulfills our needs and desires
LOVE	**PERFECT SELF-EXPRESSION**
Relationships that are fulfilling and love based	Work that fulfills our passion

RECAP

When we grasp the depth of Florence's teachings, all becomes clear. We are able to see how our thought patterns and beliefs have shaped our lives. We create the status of our relationships, finances, health, and work. We do it.

We are taught by the physical world to blame others — to be a victim. We are not victims. We are choosing — daily — what we want our lives to be.

Knowing this to be true, we are then better able to accept the fact that we can truly BE, HAVE, and DO anything we desire.

Florence Scovel Shinn was and is a truly gifted individual whose life was an example to all with whom she came into contact. You too will be an example of Florence's teachings: working in tandem with the conscious, subconscious, and superconscious minds — working as one with God/The Universal Supply Warehouse. People will be asking how you are creating the changes in your life!

In looking back at your life since you opened this workbook, you can see how your life has changed. As you have experienced these pages it is clear to see that all is not as it seems in many situations. A seeming adversity may be the stepping stone to fulfillment of your highest good, of what you desire. You've learned to bless adversity and in so doing, you have become based in love, forcing the Universe to "match" to you — more love. You can see the growth in the experiences expressed in your journal.

Continue to journal — daily if you possibly can. Your journal is a direct gateway to connecting with the Divinity within and maintaining balance of your three levels of consciousness. It always will be. Daily journaling will bring forward more and more information, more understanding, and more spiritual growth.

May you be profoundly blessed in this moment and in every moment after.

PERSONAL JOURNAL

PERSONAL JOURNAL

Perfect Self-Expression or The Divine Design

■ ■ ■ ■ ■

There is for each man perfect self-expression. There is a place which he is to fill and no one else can fill, something which he is to do, which no one else can do; it is his destiny!

This achievement is held, a perfect idea in Divine Mind, awaiting man's recognition. As the imaging faculty is the creative faculty, it is necessary for man to see the idea, before it can manifest.

So man's highest demand is for the *Divine Design of his life.*

He may not have the faintest conception of what it is, for there is, possibly, some marvelous talent, hidden deep within him.

His demand should be: *"Infinite Spirit, open the way for the Divine Design of my life to manifest; let the genius within me now be released; let me see clearly the perfect plan."*

The perfect plan includes Health, Wealth, Love, and Perfect Self-Expression. This is the *Square of Life,* which brings perfect happiness. When one has made this demand, he may find great changes taking place in his life, for nearly every man has wandered far from the Divine Design.

I know, in one woman's case, it was as though a cyclone had struck her affairs, but readjustments came quickly, and new and wonderful conditions took the place of old ones.

Perfect self-expression will never be labor; but of such absorbing interest that it will seem almost like play. The student knows, also, as man comes into the world financed by God, the *supply* needed for his perfect self-expression will be at hand.

_____

_____

_____

_____

_____

_____

_____

_____

_____

_____

_____

_____

_____

_____

Many a genius has struggled for years with the problem of supply, when his spoken word, and faith, would have released quickly, the necessary funds.

For example: After the class, one day, a man came to me and handed me a cent.

He said: "I have just seven cents in the world, and I'm going to give you one; for I have faith in the power of your spoken word. I want you to speak the word for my perfect self-expression and prosperity."

I "spoke the word," and did not see him again until a year later. He came in one day, successful and happy, with a roll of yellow bills in his pocket. He said, "Immediately after you spoke the word, I had a position offered me in a distant city, and am now demonstrating health, happiness, and supply."

A woman's perfect self-expression may be in becoming a perfect wife, a perfect mother, a perfect homemaker and not necessarily in having a public career.

Demand definite leads, and the way will be made easy and successful.

One should not visualize or force a mental picture. When he demands the Divine Design to come into his conscious mind, he will receive flashes of inspiration, and begin to see himself making some great accomplishment. This is the picture, or idea, he must hold without wavering.

The thing man seeks is seeking him — *the telephone was seeking Bell!*

Parents should never force careers and professions upon their children. With a knowledge of spiritual Truth, the divine plan could be spoken for, early in childhood, or prenatally.

A prenatal treatment should be: "Let the God in this child have perfect expression; let the Divine Design of his mind, body, and affairs be made manifest throughout his life, throughout eternity."

God's will be done, not man's; God's pattern, not man's pattern, is the command we find running through all the scriptures, and the Bible is a book dealing with the science of the mind. It is a book telling man how to release his soul (or subconscious mind) from bondage.

The battles described are pictures of man waging war against mortal thoughts. "A man's foes shall be they of his own household." Every man is Jehoshaphat, and every man is David, who slays Goliath (mortal thinking) with the little white stone (faith).

So man must be careful that his is not the "wicked and slothful servant" who buried his talent. There is a terrible penalty to be paid for not using one's ability.

Often fear stands between man and his perfect self-expression. Stage fright has hampered many a genius. This may be overcome by the spoken word or treatment. The individual then loses all self-consciousness, and feels simply that he is a channel for Infinite Intelligence to express Itself through.

He is under direct inspiration, fearless, and confident; for he feels that it is the "Father within" him who does the work.

A young boy came often to my class with his mother. He asked me to "speak the word" for his coming examinations at school.

I told him to make the statement: "I am one with Infinite Intelligence. I know everything I should know on this subject." He had an excellent knowledge of history, but was not sure of his arithmetic. I saw him afterwards, and he said: "I spoke the word for my arithmetic, and passed with the highest honors; but thought I could depend on myself for history, and got a very poor mark." Man often receives a setback when he is "too sure of himself," which means he is trusting to his personality and not the "Father within."

Another one of my students gave me an example of this. She took an extended trip abroad one summer, visiting many countries, where she was ignorant of the languages. She was calling for guidance and protection every minute, and her affairs went smoothly and miraculously. Her luggage was never delayed nor lost! Accommodations were always ready for her at the best hotels; and she had perfect service wherever she went. She returned to New York. Knowing the language, she felt God was no longer necessary, so looked after her affairs in an ordinary manner.

Everything went wrong, her trunks delayed, amid inharmony and confusion. The student must form the habit of "practicing the Presence of God" every minute. *"In all thy ways acknowledge him";* nothing is too small or too great.

Sometimes an insignificant incident may be the turning point in a man's life.

Robert Fulton, watching some boiling water, simmering in a tea kettle, saw a steamboat!

I have seen a student, often, keep back his demonstration, through resistance, or pointing the way.

He pins his faith to one channel only, and dictates just the way he desires the manifestation to come, which brings things to a standstill.

——————————————

——————————————

——————————————

——————————————

——————————————

——————————————

——————————————

——————————————

——————————————

——————————————

——————————————

——————————————

"My way, not your way!" is the command of Infinite Intelligence. Like all Power, be it steam or electricity, it must have a non-resistant engine or instrument to work through, and man is that engine or instrument.

Over and over again, man is told to "stand still." "Oh Judah, fear not; but tomorrow go out against them, for the lord will be with you. You shall not need to fight this battle; set yourselves, stand ye still, and see the salvation of the Lord with you."

We see this in the incidents of the two thousand dollars coming to the woman through the landlord when she became *non-resistant* and *undisturbed*, and the woman who won the man's love "after all suffering had ceased."

The student's goal is *Poise! Poise* is *Power*, for it gives God-Power a chance to rush through man, to "will and to do Its good pleasure."

Poised, he thinks clearly, and makes "right decisions quickly." "He never misses a trick."

Anger blurs the visions, poisons the blood, is the root of many diseases, and causes wrong decision leading to failure.

It has been named one of the worst "sins," as its reaction is so harmful. The student learns that in metaphysics sin has a much broader meaning than in the old teaching. "Whatsoever is not of faith is sin."

He finds that fear and worry are deadly sins. They are inverted faith, and through distorted mental pictures, bring to pass the thing he fears. His work is to drive out these enemies (from the subconscious mind). "When Man is fearless he is finished!" Maeterlinck says that "Man is God afraid."

So as we read in the previous chapters: man can only vanquish fear by walking up to the thing he is afraid of. When Jehoshaphat and his army prepared to meet the enemy, singing "Praise the Lord, for his mercy endureth forever," they found their enemies had destroyed each other, and there was nothing to fight.

For example: A woman asked a friend to deliver a message to another friend. The woman feared to give the message, as the reasoning mind said, "Don't get mixed up in this affair, don't give that message."

She was troubled in spirit, for she had given her promise. At last, she determined to "walk up to the lion," and call on the law of divine protection. She met the friend to whom she was to deliver the message. She opened her mouth to speak it, when her friend said, "So and So has left town." This made it unnecessary to give the message, as the situation depended upon the person being in town. As she was willing to do it, she was not obliged to; as she did not fear, the situation vanished.

The student often delays his demonstration through a belief in incompletion. He should make this statement:

"In Divine Mind there is only completion, therefore, my demonstration is completed. My perfect work, my perfect home, my perfect health." Whatever he demands are perfect ideas registered in Divine Mind, and must manifest, "under grace in a perfect way." He gives thanks he has already received on the invisible, and makes active preparation for receiving on the visible.

One of my students was in need of a financial demonstration. She came to me and asked why it was not completed.

I replied: "Perhaps you are in the habit of leaving things unfinished, and the subconscious has gotten into the habit of not completing (as the without, so the within)."

She said, "You are right. I often *begin things* and never finish them.

"I'll go home and finish something I commenced weeks ago, and I know it will be symbolic of my demonstration."

She sewed assiduously, and the article was soon completed. Shortly after, the money came in a most curious manner.

Her husband was paid his salary twice that month. He told the people of their mistake, and they sent word to keep it.

When man ask, *believing, he must receive, for God creates His own channels!*

I have been sometimes asked, "Suppose one has several talents, how is he to know which one to choose?" Demand to be shown definitely, say: "Infinite Spirit, give me a definite lead, reveal to me my perfect self-expression, show me which talent I am to make use of now."

I have known people to suddenly enter a new line of work, and be fully equipped, with little or no training. So make the statement: *"I am fully equipped for the Divine Plan of my life,"* and be fearless in grasping opportunities.

Some people are cheerful givers, but bad receivers. They refuse gifts through pride, or some negative reason, thereby blocking their channels, and invariably find themselves eventually with little or nothing. For example: A woman who had given away a great deal of money, had a gift offered her of several thousand dollars. She refused to take it, saying she did not need it. Shortly after that, her finances were "tied up," and she found herself in debt for that amount. Man should receive gracefully the bread returning to him upon the water — freely ye have given, freely ye shall receive.

There is always the perfect balance of giving and receiving, and though man should give without thinking of returns, he violates law if he does not accept the returns that come to him; for all gifts are from God, man being merely the channel.

A thought of lack should never be held over the giver.

For example: When the man gave the one cent, I did not say, "Poor man, he cannot afford to give me that." I saw him rich and prosperous, with his supply pouring in. It was this thought which brought it. If one has been a bad receiver, he must become a good one, and take even a postage stamp if it is given him, and open up his channels for receiving.

The Lord loveth a cheerful receiver, as well as a cheerful giver.

I have often been asked why one man is born rich and healthy, and another poor and sick.

Where there is an effect there is always a cause; there is no such thing as chance.

This question is answered through the law of reincarnation. Man goes through many births and deaths, until he knows the truth that sets him free.

He is drawn back to the earth plane through unsatisfied desire, to pay his Karmic debts, or to "fulfill his destiny."

The man born rich and healthy has had pictures in his subconscious mind, in his past life, of health and riches; and the poor and sick man, of disease and poverty. Man manifests, on any plane, the sum total of his subconscious beliefs.

However, birth and death are man-made laws, for the "wages of sin is death"— the Adamic fall in consciousness through the belief in *two powers*. The real man, spiritual man, is birthless and deathless! He never was born and has never died — "As he was in the beginning, he is now, and ever shall be!"

So through the truth, man is set free from the law of Karma, sin, and death, and manifests the man-made in "His image and likeness." Man's freedom comes through fulfilling his destiny, bringing into manifestation the Divine Design of his life.

His lord will say unto him: "Well done thou good and faithful servant, thou has been faithful over a few things, I will make thee ruler over many things (death itself); enter thou into the joy of thy Lord (eternal life)."

_____

_____

_____

_____

_____

_____

_____

_____

_____

_____

_____

_____

_____

WORKBOOK SESSION NINE

Perfect Self-Expression or The Divine Design

Topics:

- Divine Life Path
- Financed by God
- Demand a Lead

- We Are Non-Resistant Instruments
- The Cheerful Receiver — Balance of Giving and Receiving
- Recap and Personal Journal

Begin this session by breathing deeply to achieve balance. Surround yourself with God's Divine White Light of Protection and set your intention to connect with your Higher Self.

Father, Mother, God, Creator of All That Is...

I claim my personal power and open the way to see clearly my Field of Potentiality, my field of infinite possibilities. I cut the ties of beliefs and thought patterns that no longer serve me in all directions of time, removing them from my consciousness, my subconscious, and my superconscious. I fearlessly step into the magnificence of the true essence of who I am — One with God. I graciously accept all that is mine by Divine Right, under grace in a miraculous way and commit to fulfill all that I came to be, have, and do in this incarnation on Mother Earth at this time.

Amen

Ask your guides, angels, and teachers to be present with you to help you open your heart, mind, and spirit to the infinite possibilities of you.

DIVINE LIFE PATH

Chapter 9, Perfect Self-Expression or The Divine Design, is a beacon of light to understanding even more of who we are and why we are here.

Each one of us is a uniquely gifted spiritual being, the only one who can fill our space in the physical world of earth. Each one of us asks, "What is my mission? What is my Divine Life Path?"

When we set our intention for change and demand it, the old energy shifts and change begins whether we see it or not. Sometimes we get scared of change and we pull our intention back and negate our demand by plunging headlong back into fear.

This is normal because we begin to get a glimpse of something different — the results of changing energy is outside our box and the physical world conditioned part of us gets frightened. We must let this fear of something new, the unknown, go in order to change our lives from what we've been living to something new.

Florence shares with us this demand for guidance to perfect self-expression: "Infinite Spirit, open the way for the Divine Design of my life to manifest; let the genius within me now be released; let me see clearly the perfect plan."

 INSIDE ASSIGNMENT

Where Am I? This exercise is designed to help you discern your location in your Divine Life Path. Sit quietly and breathe deeply and completely.

Set the intention and connect with your Higher Self and honestly review your life path. Review what you have been doing and what you desire to do. You may use the bonus gift: Tap into Your Higher Self at www.GameOfLifeMastery.com/freegift.

Each time you experience this connection you will learn more about yourself and the path of your life. Address any resistance that is revealed. Use the Personal Journal to write about your experiences and your developing life path.

FINANCED BY GOD

What would your life look like if you believed you are financed by God?

Physical world conditioning teaches us that we are limited by circumstances, environment, race, cultures, and locality. We are only truly limited if we believe this conditioning. In reality we are gifted, limitless spiritual beings experiencing a human existence connected to everyone else by the divinity within us. As profoundly loved children of God our birthright is to live in prosperous abundance in all areas of our lives. It is our birthright.

In 1988 four men from Jamaica and their coach entered the Olympic Winter Games in Calgary. They entered the bobsledding event. There is no snow in Jamaica to practice bobsledding. The physical world "reasoning mind" would tell us their entering the event was absurd. However, they qualified and they raced. In the 1992 Winter Olympics the team finished fourteenth, stunning their critics. In 1993 Disney immortalized the Jamaican bobsledding team in the movie *Cool Runnings*.

Like the Jamaican bobsledders, we too are Limitless Spiritual Beings…

Florence teaches us that the world is financed by God. God is the Universal Supply Warehouse — the All That Is. She also teaches us that our "perfect self-expression," our work, "will never be labor; but of such absorbing interest that it will seem almost like play." When we love what we do our work is like play!

In following our guidance to our perfect self-expression we may be led to surprising locations, services, etc. But when we follow these leads, these hunches, our intuition, we find our true happiness and joy in the service that we give to the world. In working with our conscious, subconscious, and superconscious, we also discover that monies needed to support us are provided — often times miraculously.

DEMAND A LEAD

We have the choice to struggle and flail around in our physical world life on our own or to work with God/the Universe to create the life we really desire.

Every day we choose to live our lives from a source of fear or a source of love. Every day we make this choice. The physical world is full of pitfalls, tests, trials, and challenges. It is what we do with the energy of these challenges that define who we are and create our reality. It is the wise spiritual being who demands (formally claims) leads (guidance). The guidance is ours, all we have to do is connect with it, open our heart to understand it, and then act on it.

As humans we question ourselves on just about everything. When it comes to something we really want to experience in our lives, we can become fanatical in questioning ourselves. This is the perfect time to "demand a lead" — to be shown we are on the right path to manifesting our desire.

44 ▸ INSIDE ASSIGNMENT

What Would I Do? In embracing the knowledge that you are "financed by God" anything is possible. The next question is, "What would I do if I knew I could not fail?"

Take just a moment and ponder this question. What immediately pops into your head? Did your mind go blank? A lot of the fear that has prevented you from dreaming should now be gone.

Read the questions carefully, and then allow yourself to connect with your Higher Self within before writing your answers.

What would my life look like if every aspect was filled with prosperity?

_____

_____

What would I do if I knew I could not fail?

_____

_____

What can I do today to bring the life of my dreams into my reality?

_____

_____

What can I do this month to bring the life of my dreams into reality?

_____

_____

What can I do this year to bring the life of my dreams into reality?

_____

_____

Work on one area of your life at a time so as not to overwhelm yourself. Use the Personal Journal to write about how you felt doing this exercise.

WE ARE NON-RESISTANT INSTRUMENTS

God is our supply in all things — including the air that we breathe. We don't worry that there will be enough air — it isn't a concern. We don't try to control it; the air simply flows around us and in us through our breath. We are non-resistant to the air.

As discussed before, we humans have a tendency to want to "control" everything. This need to control events, conditions, situations, and people places a wall of resistance within us and blocks universal flow. Resistance is a negative, fear-based action/emotion.

Florence teaches us to become a non-resistant instrument, to allow God to work through us. Achieving this state of trust and faith not only unlocks the doors of prosperous abundance for each area of our life, it nails them open!

The example Florence used of the woman who was traveling abroad shows us that while the woman was working in tandem with God, trusting that God would be her supply, she was non-resistant. Her non-resistance allowed God/the Universe to provide for her. The moment she took control of her affairs, she put up a wall of resistance, thereby stopping the flow of God's supply.

Becoming a non-resistant instrument allows our universal supply to flow to us freely — as with the air that surrounds us.

In setting the intent to be non-resistant to the events, conditions, situations, and people around us, we base ourselves in love — as One with God. We exhibit that we are trusting and in faith of God's wisdom. As a result, we are able to think clearly to discern our next action without the hindrance of fear-based emotions of resistance getting in our way.

Being non-resistant does NOT mean that we do not care. The act of non-resistance is our trust and faith in God as our supply.

THE CHEERFUL RECEIVER — BALANCE OF GIVING AND RECEIVING

Florence tells us: "Man should receive gracefully the bread returning to him upon the water — freely ye have given, freely ye shall receive. There is always the perfect balance of giving and receiving, and though man should give without thinking of returns, he violates law if he does not accept the returns that come to him; for all gifts are from God, man being merely the channel."

Many of us give and give and give and give of ourselves. It is who we are and this is okay. Yet in order to live a balanced life, we must also be a cheerful receiver. Since we are all connected as one, we are both the giver and the receiver.

This concept can be tricky. Giving to others is of love. In giving to others we graciously receive the inner warmth of giving. In allowing ourselves to graciously receive from others, we graciously give back to them the flow of love. It is a full-circle event.

However, if we stop someone from giving to us, we block their flow as well as our own.

Florence gives the example of accepting the penny from the man who had only seven cents to his name. She did not see him as a poor man, but as a rich and prosperous man — and so he was. Had she denied his gift to her she would not only have stopped his flow, but hers as well.

Graciously and cheerfully receive what the Universe sends to you. This is your part in the flow of universal abundance to not only yourself, but to others. None of us wants to be the block for someone else — practice gracious, cheerful receiving!

INSIDE ASSIGNMENT

Cheerful Receiver This exercise is designed to discover if you are a cheerful receiver. Read each question carefully and answer it honestly.

1. You receive a check in the mail for $1.50. Do you cash it or throw it away?

_____

_____

2. A friend who has very little offers to share with you. Do you see him in the light of Powerful Master Creator and graciously thank him, or do you see him as less than prosperous and decline?

_____

_____

3. You receive a compliment. Do you negate the love of the gesture or do you graciously receive it and say thank you?

_____

_____

4. You have lunch with a friend and she offers to pay for lunch. Do you graciously accept or insist on paying for your half?

_____

_____

Each of these events are gifts from the Universe — any time we are in receipt of something, it is a gift from the Universe. To encourage universal flow of abundance, the answer is to graciously accept each gift. Use the Personal Journal to write about any past examples of being a gracious receiver or blocking your receipt.

RECAP

What does fear and worry do to enhance your life? Living a life in fear and worry is a choice. What you continually focus on will manifest in your life. This question and these statements together are life changing.

Clearly, you've made the decision to change your life and live from love source — you have continued the workbook. Incorporating love-based thought patterns and beliefs into your conscious, subconscious, and superconscious has changed your life.

You can't go back. Now you have a firm grasp on the laws of the Universe, and how to use them to create your highest good as the reality of your life.

The physical world can be a harsh place, yet with this blossoming of inner knowing, it is easier to focus on the beauty and the love that the physical world can offer and add your love source energy to the shift of the collective consciousness.

Your journal is a priceless tool of support and guidance to help you stay on track.

Be sure to thank your angelic entourage for being in attendance and helping you to clearly understand God's work and guidance.

May you be profoundly blessed in this moment and in every moment after.

PERSONAL JOURNAL

PERSONAL JOURNAL

CHAPTER 10

Denials and Affirmations

■ ■ ■ ■ ■

All the good that is to be made manifest in man's life is already an accomplished fact in Divine Mind, and is released through man's recognition, or spoken word, so he must be careful to decree that only the Divine Idea be made manifest, for often, he decrees, through his "idle words," failure, or misfortune.

It is, therefore, of the utmost importance, to word one's demands correctly, as stated in a previous chapter.

If one desires a home, friend, position, or any other good thing, make the demand for the "divine selection."

For example: "Infinite Spirit, open the way for my right home, my right friend, my right position. I give thanks *it now manifests under grace in a perfect way.*"

The latter part of the statement is most important. For example: I knew a woman who demanded a thousand dollars. Her daughter was injured and they received a thousand dollars indemnity, so it did not come in a "perfect way."

The demand should have been worded in this way: "Infinite Spirit, I give thanks that the one thousand dollars, which is mine by Divine Right, is now released, and reaches me under grace in a perfect way."

As one grows in a financial consciousness, he should demand that the enormous sums of money, which are his by Divine Right, reach him under grace, in perfect ways.

It is impossible for man to release more than he thinks is possible, for one is bound by the limited expectancies of the subconscious. He must enlarge his expectancies in order to receive in a larger way.

Man so often limits himself in his demands. For example: A student made the demand for six hundred dollars, by a certain date. He did receive it, but heard afterwards, that he came very near receiving a thousand dollars, but he was given just six hundred, as the result of his spoken word.

"They limited the Holy One of Israel." Wealth is a matter of consciousness. The French have a legend giving an example of this. A poor man was walking along a road when he met a traveler, who stopped him and said: "My good friend, I see you are poor. Take this gold nugget, sell it, and you will be rich all your days."

The man was overjoyed at his good fortune, and took the nugget home. He immediately found work and became so prosperous that he did not sell the nugget. Years passed, and he became a very rich man. One day he met a poor man on the road. He stopped him and said: "My good friend, I will give you this gold nugget, which, if you sell, will make you rich for life." The mendicant took the nugget, had it valued, and found it was only brass. So we see, the first man became rich through feeling rich, thinking the nugget was gold.

Every man has within himself a gold nugget; *it is his consciousness of gold, of opulence, which brings riches into his life.* In making his demands, man begins at his *journey's end*, that is he declares *he has already received.* "*Before* ye call I shall answer."

Continually affirming establishes the belief in the subconscious.

It would not be necessary to make an affirmation more than once if one had perfect faith! One should not plead or supplicate, but give thanks repeatedly, that he has received.

"The desert shall *rejoice* and blossom as the rose." This rejoicing which is yet in the desert (state of consciousness) opens the way for release. The Lord's Prayer is in the form of command and demand, "Give us this day our daily bread, and forgive us our debts as we forgive our debtors," and ends in praise, "For thine is the Kingdom and the Power and the Glory, forever. Amen." "Concerning the works of my hands, command ye me." So prayer is command and demand, praise and thanksgiving. The student's work is in making himself believe that "with God all things are possible."

This is easy enough to state in the abstract, but a little more difficult when confronted with a problem. For example: It was necessary for a woman to demonstrate a large sum of money within a stated time. She knew she must *do something* to get a realization (for realization is manifestation), and she demanded a "lead."

She was walking through a department store, when she saw a very beautiful pink enamel paper cutter. She felt the "pull" towards it. The thought came. "I haven't a paper cutter good enough to open letters containing large cheques."

So she bought the paper cutter, which the reasoning mind would have called an extravagance. When she held it in her hand, she had a flash of a picture of herself opening an envelope containing a large cheque, and in a few weeks, she received the money. The pink paper cutter was her bridge of active faith.

Many stories are told of the power of the subconscious when directed in faith.

For example: A man was spending the night in a farmhouse. The windows of the room had been nailed down, and in the middle of the night he felt suffocated and made his way in the dark to the window. He could not open it, so he smashed the pane with his fist, drew in draughts of fine fresh air, and had a wonderful night's sleep.

The next morning, he found he had smashed the glass of a bookcase and the window had remained closed during the whole night. He had *supplied himself with oxygen, simply by his thought of oxygen.*

When a student starts out to demonstrate, he should never turn back. "Let not that man who wavers think that he shall receive anything of the Lord."

A student once made this wonderful statement, "When I ask the Father for anything, I put my foot down, and I say: Father, I'll take nothing less than I've asked for, but more!" So man should never compromise: "Having done all — Stand." This is sometimes the most difficult time of demonstrating. The temptation comes to give up, to turn back, to compromise.

"He also serves who only stands and waits."

Demonstrations often come at the eleventh hour because man then lets go, that is, stops reasoning, and Infinite Intelligence has a chance to work.

"Man's dreary desires are answered drearily, and his impatient desires, long delayed or violently fulfilled.

For example: A woman asked me why it was she was constantly losing or breaking her glasses.

We found she often said to herself and others with vexation, "I wish I could get rid of my glasses." So her impatient desire was violently fulfilled. What she should have demanded was perfect eyesight, but what she registered in the subconscious was simply the impatient desire to be rid of her glasses; so they were continually being broken or lost.

Two attitudes of mind cause loss: *depreciation*, as in the case of the woman who did not appreciate her husband, *or fear of loss*, which makes a picture of loss in the subconscious.

When a student is able to let go of his problem (cast his burden) he will have instantaneous manifestation.

For example: A woman was out during a very stormy day and her umbrella was blown inside-out. She was about to make a call on some people whom she had never met and she did not wish to make her first appearance with a dilapidated umbrella. She could not throw it away, as it did not belong to her. So in desperation, she exclaimed: "Oh God, you take charge of this umbrella, I don't know what to do."

A moment later, a voice behind her said: "Lady, do you want your umbrella mended?" There stood an umbrella mender.

She replied, "Indeed, I do."

The man mended the umbrella, while she went into the house to pay her call, and when she returned, she had a good umbrella. So there is always an umbrella mender at hand, on man's pathway, when one puts the umbrella (or situation) in God's hands.

One should always follow a denial with an affirmation.

For example: I was called on the phone late one night to treat a man whom I had never seen. He was apparently very ill. I made the statement: "I deny this appearance of disease. It is unreal, therefore cannot register in his consciousness; this man is a perfect idea in Divine Mind, pure substance expressing perfection."

There is no time or space, in Divine Mind, therefore the word reaches instantly its destination and does not "return void." I have treated patients in Europe and have found that the results were instantaneous.

I am asked so often the difference between visualizing and visioning. Visualizing is a mental process governed by the reasoning or conscious mind; visioning is a spiritual process, governed by intuition, or the superconscious mind. The student should train his mind to receive these flashes of inspiration, and work out the "divine pictures," through definite leads. When a man can say, "I desire only that which God desires for me," his new set of blueprints is given him by the Master Architect, the God within. God's plan for each man transcends the limitation of the reasoning mind, and is always the Square of Life, containing Health, Wealth, Love, and Perfect Self-Expression. Many a man is building for himself in imagination a bungalow when he should be building a palace.

If a student tries to force a demonstration (through the reasoning mind) he brings it to a standstill. "I will hasten it," saith the Lord. He should act only through intuition, or definite leads. "Rest in the Lord and wait patiently. Trust also in him, and he will bring it to pass."

I have seen the law work in the most astonishing manner. For example: A student stated that it was necessary for her to have a hundred dollars for the following day. It was a debt of vital importance which had to be met. I "spoke the word," declaring Spirit was "never too late" and that the supply was at hand.

That evening she phoned me of the miracle. She said that the thought came to her to go to her safe-deposit box at the bank to examine some papers. She looked over the papers, and at the bottom of the box, was a new one hundred dollar bill. She was astounded, and said she knew she had never put it there, for she had gone through the papers many times. It may have been a materialization, as Jesus Christ materialized the loaves and fishes.

Man will reach the stage in which his "word is made flesh," or materialized, instantly. "The fields, ripe with the harvest" will manifest immediately, as in all of the miracles of Jesus Christ.

There is a tremendous power alone in the name Jesus Christ. It stands for *Truth Made Manifest*. He said, "Whatsoever ye ask the Father, in my name, he will give it to you."

The power of this name raises the student into the fourth dimension, where he is freed from all astral and psychic influences, and he becomes "unconditioned and absolute, as God Himself is unconditioned and absolute."

I have seen many healings accomplished by using the words, "In the name of Jesus Christ."

Christ was both person and principle; and the Christ within each man is his Redeemer and Salvation.

The Christ within is his own fourth dimensional self, the man made in God's image and likeness. This is the self that has never failed, never known sickness or sorrow, was never born and has never died. It is the "resurrection and the life" of each man! "No man cometh to the Father save by the Son," means, that God, the Universal, working on the place of the particular, becomes the Christ in man; and the Holy Ghost, means God in-action. So daily, man is manifesting the Trinity of Father, Son, and Holy Ghost.

Man should make an art of thinking. The Master Thinker is an artist and is careful to paint only the divine designs upon the canvas of his mind; and he paints these pictures with masterly strokes of power and decision, having perfect faith that there is no power to mar their perfection and that they shall manifest in his life the ideal made real.

All power is given man (through right thinking) to bring *his heaven* upon *his earth,* and this is the *goal of The Game of Life.*

The simple rules are fearless faith, non-resistance, and love!

May each reader be now freed from that thing which has held him in bondage through the ages, standing between him and his own, and "know the Truth which makes him free" — free to fulfill his destiny, to bring into manifestation the *"Divine Design of his life,* Health, Wealth, Love, and Perfect Self-Expression." "Be ye transformed by the renewing of your mind."

DENIALS AND AFFIRMATIONS

For Prosperity: *God is my unfailing supply, and large sums of money come to me quickly, under grace, in perfect ways.*

For Right Conditions: *Every plan my Father in heaven has not planned shall be dissolved and dissipated, and the Divine Idea now comes to pass.*

For Right Conditions: *Only that which is true of God is true of me, for I and the Father are ONE.*

For Faith: *As I am one with God, I am one with my good, for God is both the Giver and the Gift. I cannot separate the Giver from the gift.*

For Right Conditions: *Divine Love now dissolves and dissipates every wrong condition in my mind, body, and affairs. Divine Love is the most powerful chemical in the Universe, and dissolves everything which is not of itself!*

For Health: *Divine Love floods my consciousness with health, and every cell in my body is filled with light.*

For the Eyesight: *My eyes are God's eyes, I see with the eyes of spirit. I see clearly the open way; there are no obstacles on my pathway. I see clearly the perfect plan.*

For Guidance: *I am divinely sensitive to my intuitive leads, and give instant obedience to Thy will.*

For the Hearing: *My ears are God's ears, I hear with the ears of spirit. I am non-resistant and am willing to be led. I hear glad tidings of great joy.*

For Right Work: *I have a perfect work in a perfect way, I give a perfect service for perfect pay.*

For Freedom from all Bondage: *I cast this burden on the Christ within, and I go free!*

WORKBOOK SESSION TEN

Denials and Affirmations

Topics:

- Manifesting under Grace in a Perfect Way

- Limiting Thoughts and Beliefs Versus Achieving a Feeling of Opulence

- The Power of Gratitude

- Releasing to God

- Visualizing and Visioning

- Fearless Faith, Non-Resistance, and Love!

- Recap and Personal Journal

Begin this session by breathing deeply to achieve balance. Surround yourself with God's Divine White Light of Protection and set your intention to connect with your Higher Self.

Father, Mother, God, Creator of All That Is…

I claim my personal power and open the way to see clearly my Field of Potentiality, my field of infinite possibilities. I cut the ties of beliefs and thought patterns that no longer serve me in all directions of time, removing them from my consciousness, my subconscious, and my superconscious. I fearlessly step into the magnificence of the true essence of who I am — One with God. I graciously accept all that is mine by Divine Right, under grace in a miraculous way and commit to fulfill all that I came to be, have, and do in this incarnation on Mother Earth at this time.

Amen

Ask your guides, angels, and teachers to be present with you to help you open your heart, mind, and spirit to the infinite possibilities of you.

MANIFESTING UNDER GRACE IN A PERFECT WAY

At this time in the twenty-first century the veil is thinning at an accelerated rate and we are able to manifest what we desire or don't desire very quickly.

While finalizing this workbook my daughter shared a very interesting experience. She leaned forward and whispered to me that she has "power," then proceeded to explain. She's been using visualization to direct her two-year-old papipoo dog, Jayden. When she goes to bed she visualizes where she wants him to lay on the bed, then when he gets settled she'll visualize another place, so he gets up and moves to the other place. Then she'll visualize yet another place and again he moves to the new place.

When she explained this to me she emphasized making the visualization an immediate picture, then going on to think about something else. The puppy would pick up the thought directed at him and move accordingly.

When my daughter "visualized" what she wanted Jayden to do she was fully in the moment in love source. The veil between the physical world and the world of Divine Mind is parting and we ARE manifesting quickly. It is more important now than ever before in the history of man to monitor closely how we exert energy.

The question of "Can we manifest our desires?" has been answered. The instant of being "in the moment" and making a decision is all it takes to manifest into our reality. The time is upon us. Now the question is "what are we going to do with this power?"

We've learned that all thoughts, words, and actions are either of love source or fear source — there is no in between. We've also learned that the Law of Attraction works for both love and fear. When we are living from a love source, we attract more love. When we are living from a fear source, we attract more fear. The Universe makes no distinction as to whether our focus is love based or fear based — its job is to match to us the same vibrational frequency that we put out.

Therefore if we are not truly in love source, if there is fear involved, what we demand may be matched to us from fear source. The woman who demanded one-thousand dollars and received it as an indemnity payment from her daughter's accident is a perfect example of this.

Florence states that "All the good that is to be made manifest in life is already an accomplished fact in Divine Mind, and is released through recognition, or spoken word."

She takes the application of this law a step further by

teaching us to formally claim/demand the divine selection to come to us "under grace in a perfect way."

Her affirmation is: "Infinite Spirit, open the way for my right home, my right friend, my right position. I give thanks it now manifests under grace in a perfect way."

Manifesting "under grace in a perfect way" seals the deal to make manifest what we desire for the highest good of everyone.

Could manifesting what we desire be this easy?

Yes, it is this easy.

In the prior workbook session we explored what we would do if we "knew" we could not fail. The fact is that anything is possible. If we dream about something it's in our Field of Potentiality. It has yet to manifest in our lives because we blocked the manifestation. There is nothing outside of us blocking manifestation. What blocks us is the fear within.

Limiting Thoughts and Beliefs Versus Achieving a State of Opulence

We've learned that the physical world conditions/teaches us to believe that we are limited in everything. Limited in what we can be, have, or do. We've learned that the reality is that we are limitless spiritual beings that can be, have, or do anything.

As we have elevated our vibrational frequency to a state of love, we have experienced the feeling of opulence. It is easy for us to distinguish between the two — fear-based limitedness and love-based limitlessness/opulence. We have experienced the full spectrum — the lower vibrational frequency of fear and the higher vibrational frequency of love — we know what the duality feels like deep within our core.

 INSIDE ASSIGNMENT

Red Flag This exercise is designed to help you recognize limiting thought patterns and beliefs when they happen so you may immediately change them from fear energy to love energy. Read the situation, and then recognize what your immediate feelings/thoughts are.

RECOGNIZING SNEAKY LIMITING/FEAR-BASED THOUGHTS

1. Your car is at least ten years old and has well over 100,000 miles on it. You've been admiring another newer model. You see an advertisement of the vehicle at a reduced price. Your immediate thought is:

   a.   I can't afford that.

   b.   I can have this car!

2. You are in a relationship and you see two people walking hand-in-hand. Your immediate thought is:

   a.   I never do that with my spouse/partner.

   b.   I have a feeling of gratitude and love for

       my spouse/partner.

3. You are not in a relationship and you see two people walking hand-in-hand. Your immediate thought is:

   a.   I'm always alone.

   b.   I feel the love and gratitude swell within my

       heart at the possibilities of the future!

4. A co-worker gets an unexpected promotion. Your immediate thought is:

   a.   Why doesn't anything good happen to me?

   b.   My heart swells with happiness for the co-worker!

5   You're walking down the street and the person behind you finds a ten-dollar bill on the sidewalk. Your immediate thought is:

   a.   Why didn't I see that?

   b.   I feel joy for the good fortune of the person!

Use the Personal Journal to write about what you discovered about yourself. Did you immediately think a or b consistently? If you chose a, please identify the basis for the negative reaction and work with the tools you have learned to release them. If you chose b, congratulations. You are living from a source of love!

THE POWER OF GRATITUDE

Gratitude is the key to unlocking the vault of joy. When we examine the feelings within our body when we experience gratitude, it is easy to understand how powerful gratitude is.

We live in a harsh third dimensional physical world. The state of gratitude gives us a firm grip on our power. When we stay in the joy of gratitude, we block the fear of the physical world from hurting us. It is as a shield of armor that is very powerful!

BEING in the state of gratitude is love source so the Universe matches to us more to be grateful for!

The next exercise is designed to create Gratitude Attraction Magnets. These Gratitude Attraction Magnets will be used when you recognize fear-based thoughts interfering in your love-based world. You'll be able to use these Attraction Magnets to transmute the fear-based thoughts to love.

 47 ▸ I N S I D E   A S S I G N M E N T

Forever Grateful List at least six things, people, or experiences (more if you can) that you feel opulently grateful for when you think about them.

GRATITUDE ATTRACTION MAGNETS

1. _____

2. _____

3. _____

4. _____

5. _____

6. _____

7. _____

8. _____

9. _____

10. _____

During the next week write in your journal each time you use your Gratitude Attraction Magnets. Notice how quickly you are able to move from fear energy to love energy.

RELEASING TO GOD

As we have proceeded through this workbook and Florence's book we've learned of the power of releasing people/conditions/situations to God — the power of forgiveness and the power of non-resistance.

We are each a spiritual being, but we are also human. The human side of us does not want to let go or to release our control of people, conditions, or situations to anybody — especially not to someone we cannot see. How can we trust God to take care of anything?

The definition of human should include "control freak." We continually work at controlling and judging every little thing. It is what we are taught to do as a society. Shifting into a state of love and allowing changes everything. When our children do something we don't approve of, they feel our judgment on them and our need to control their actions. This creates disharmony whether we "say" anything or not because our thoughts are energy, just like our words.

Florence shares with us the story of the lady whose umbrella was blown inside-out. She turned the situation over to God, verbally, by saying "Oh God, you take charge of this umbrella, I don't know what to do." Immediately God provided someone to help her with the umbrella.

We find it easy to hand over to God parking spaces, but when it comes to important things like finding a new place to live or a new job, we tend to shut God out and try to manifest what we desire from fear source.

Remember, "God helps those who help themselves" doesn't mean we must do everything on our own. It means "God helps those who have the faith and trust in Him to give our desires to Him to fulfill."

VISUALIZING AND VISIONING

Florence explains visualizing and visioning in the following manner:

Visualizing is a mental process governed by the reasoning or conscious mind.

Visioning is a spiritual process, governed by intuition, or the superconscious mind.

As we progress in our bonding connection with our Higher Self within through meditation and quiet conversations, we will become privy to visions of our gifts and/or our mission. We will be guided to steps to take to bring the visions into our reality.

Visualizing is a powerful tool to manifest our desires. Visualizing what we truly desire in our lives will anchor it in the Universe, giving the Universe a clear understanding of the vibrational frequency that it must match.

Our ability to manifest into our lives what we desire is quickly escalating. Florence gives a wonderful example of a tangible physical world tool with the story of the "golden nugget." The energy the first man associated with the "nugget" was of prosperous abundance, opulence. Possessing the "nugget" shifted him from deep within from the energy of lack to the energy of prosperity and he visualized his prosperity into his reality.

When we release the fear from our hearts we're then able to shift to a state of "possibility." We move the energy and our life changes. We're able to draw to us and manifest into our reality that which we desire.

48 ▶ I N S I D E   A S S I G N M E N T

Unlimited Vision This exercise is designed to help you expand your feelings of limitlessness and experience in your mind the desires of your heart.

VISUALIZATION FORM

1. Get clear on what you want to create. Visualize the experience of being, doing, and having what you want. Visualize how it feels, how it looks, what it tastes like, what you look like wearing it, how it smells. Is it cold? Is it hot? Visualize experiencing your desire with all your senses. Write about what you desire here — be specific in detail.

_____

_____

_____

_____

_____

2. List some visions of receipt that your superconscious allowed you to see.

_____

_____

_____

_____

_____

_____

3. On a scale of one to ten with one being "couldn't get there" and ten being "fully experienced the joy and power of receipt," where did your experience of receiving your desire fall? If it is less than ten, repeat number 2 until it is a ten. Experience the gratitude of the visualization.

1   2   3   4   5   6   7   8   9   10
NOTHING   TOTALLY

4. Spend a few minutes each day visualizing the joy and gratitude of experiencing receipt of what you want to create or something better. Use the scale to monitor your level of receipt energy to help you stay in the highest vibration of Creation/Receipt Energy possible.

1   2   3   4   5   6   7   8   9   10
NOTHING   TOTALLY

Use the Personal Journal to write of this experience. Write about the outcome. Did you bring to fruition your desire? Or did you negate it with doubt and worry? Write about what you learned.

FEARLESS FAITH, NON-RESISTANCE, AND LOVE!

Florence's goal in *The Game of Life* is to help us free our-selves of physical world conditioning and beliefs. She set forth guidelines, examples, and now through this workbook, tools of experiential exercises to realign our three levels of consciousness.

The tools are here to bring into manifestation the Divine Design of Life, Health, Wealth, Love and Perfect Self-Expression.

49 ▶ INSIDE ASSIGNMENT

Square of Life Today This is the final exercise. You have experienced profound spiritual growth. Look at your Square of Life honestly. Read each section and write in the status of each. What does it reveal today?

Compare this form to the one in Chapter 1. How is your life different? Have you grown tremendously? Are your desires coming to fruition? Do you have more love, more peace, and more contentment in your life? Are you freer? Do you need additional support to tap into and focus your Creation Energy? Go to www.GameOfLifeMastery.com to learn more about The Game of Life Mastery Program. Use the Personal Journal to write about your discoveries.

SQUARE OF LIFE TODAY

HEALTH	**WEALTH**
A healthy physical body that houses our spirit	Cash flow that fulfills our needs and desires
LOVE	**PERFECT SELF-EXPRESSION**
Relationships that are fulfilling and love based	Work that fulfills our passion

RECAP

Now we know that aligning the energy of our thoughts and words is more. Our bodies and spiritual selves are meticulously working to align with the higher vibrational energies that are affecting our planet. We have a front-row seat to the transformation of our planet from a place of the lower vibration of fear to the higher vibration of love. It is happening, the question is, are we going to experience it kicking and screaming, being dragged along every step of the way, or are we going to step fully into our power in love source and flow in ease and grace.

As we've discussed before, the energy of Mother Earth no longer supports the darkness of fear. Mother Earth is shifting from deep within to belch out man's fear. To some this appears to be a very frightening state of affairs. The reality is that this time, we are experiencing what we've all dreamed of — a time to live in love and light and manifest our heart's desires, at times almost instantaneously.

Some are not ready for this and we must be allowing of their decision and growth. However, do not allow others to hold you back. Make yourself a priority. Evolve to the highest state of love that you possibly can in order to create your version of Heaven on Earth.

This time of transformation is to a place of love, joy, and fun. We are experiencing a metamorphosis of energy into love source where we are leaving the dark fear of the physical world behind — bringing heaven to earth.

The Inside Assignments have revealed yet more resistance within for you to heal in order to solidly anchor the New Normal of love source. You can never go back to living in the blanket of fear that has been your "normal state" all your life and lifetimes. You've opened the way for the higher vibration of love to BE your New Normal.

Acknowledge the challenges of the physical world and be aware that the illusion of fear will attempt to pull you down.

You are human and this does happen, but you will now recognize it and have the power to stop fear in its tracks!

Step back and allow yourself to see the drama for what it is — the illusion of fear.

The only true reality is love, and love doesn't hurt. There is no fear or pain in love source energy.

Be sure to thank your angelic entourage for being in attendance and helping you to shift your energy and understand how limitless you truly are!

May you be profoundly blessed in this moment and in every moment after.

PERSONAL JOURNAL

PERSONAL JOURNAL

Your Life Has Been Changed Forever

■ ■ ■ ■ ■

Your life has changed forever. You'll never be able to go back to being the "follow the leader" person who floats around on the sea of life with no direction, choking on fear. Now you have tools to claim your power and create the life you truly desire to live.

Every time you pick up this workbook you will learn more, for you will be at a higher level of evolvement and will understand yet more of the true essence of the work. Personally I've picked up *The Game of Life* hundreds of times and each time I learn more and "get" what Florence is teaching at a greater depth. The experience is always nothing short of miraculous.

This workbook holds tools of tremendous power — use them!

You are a magnificent, limitless, profoundly loved spiritual being with a Field of Potentiality and possibilities that will leave you in awe when you open your heart to tap into it. Nothing is too big or too good for you — remember this! If you need more help in maintaining your flow of love energy, you may learn more about The Game of Life Mastery Program by going to www.GameOfLifeMastery.com.

Go forth and be the spiritual being Mother Earth desires, living prosperously from a source of love...

May you be profoundly blessed in this moment and in every moment after.

In love and light,
Kate

ABOUT THE AUTHOR

Kate Large founded Soul Kisses Spiritual Whispers in 2000 as an online resource for healing and spiritual growth at a time when spiritual websites were few and far between. In January of 2003 she published her first newsletter; it now circles Mother Earth touching, healing, and illuminating the pathway for people in more than fifty countries.

She is the author of the Amazon best-seller *Waiting in the Other Room* and the host of the internationally popular Blog Talk Radio show: Spiritual Whispers with Kate Large. She is the creator of many best-selling transformational classes, meditations, and programs — including the extraordinary Game of Life Mastery Program and the Alzheimer's Alternative Care Program.

Kate is a spiritual practitioner and teacher of hope and infinite possibility. Through her teachings, she holds the space for members of the Soul Kisses community, to reconnect with their angelic entourage of Higher Self, angels, teachers, guides and deceased loved ones. Kate believes creating your version of Heaven on Earth — your most excellent Square of Life and everything in between — is not only possible, but your birthright. *Her classes, programs, and meditations have helped thousands around the world connect with the life force energy of love within them to transform their lives in magical, beautiful ways to create their version of Heaven on Earth.*

To become a member of the Soul Kisses Community and access your physical world tools to experience transformation and expansion into a higher state of being, go to www.SoulKisses.com.

THE SEDONA METHOD® OF RELEASE

This procedure is shockingly simple and extremely powerful! It is based upon The Sedona Method® releasing technique, a simple way to let go of any negative thoughts, feelings, or emotions that may arise and is printed with permission of Sedona Training Associates, Sedona.com. The purpose of the following procedure is to release completely negative beliefs and/or thought patterns that are blocking your receipt of abundance from God.

Make yourself comfortable; ask your guides and angels to surround you with God's Divine White Light. Breathe slowly and deeply to help you focus within.

The following exercise is based upon The Sedona Method® and is printed with permission of Sedona Training Associates, Sedona.com

Step 1: Focus on one of the negative beliefs or thought patterns you have about yourself that you discovered in the previous exercise. Allow yourself to experience and feel FULLY the negativity of the belief or thought pattern. Embrace the negative feelings of the belief or thought pattern. Welcome the negativity into your body freely and completely.

It sounds counter productive to "embrace" something that you are trying to "release," but it isn't. By fearlessly embracing the negative beliefs and thought patterns, you show active faith of your safety within God — you are facing your fears. You are actually releasing the negativity by embracing it into the Higher Self within you!

Step 2: Ask yourself: Could I let this feeling go? Answer the question honestly with the first answer that comes to you — "yes" or "no." No matter what the answer, try again to embrace the feeling to you — can you find the feeling? Embrace it to you. Go on to Step 3 no matter how you answered the question.

Step 3: Ask yourself: Would I let this feeling go? Answer the question honestly with the first answer that comes to you — "yes" or "no." No matter what the answer, try again to embrace the feeling to you — can you still find the feeling within you? If so, embrace it to you. Go on to Step 4 no matter how you answered the question.

Step 4: Ask yourself: When will I let this feeling go? Answer the question honestly. This question gives you the opportunity to completely dissipate the feeling NOW.

Step 5: Repeat this procedure as often as necessary to be completely free of the negativity.

It stands to reason that when your goal is to release the negative feeling, you would try to release it, not embrace it. However, in executing the act of "embracing" the feeling, you are actually releasing it through the Higher Self within you. Through the Higher Self, the negativity dissipates in Love.

Move through each section of the Square of Life releasing negative feelings with The Sedona Method® of Release. Write in your journal the negative belief or thought pattern and your experience releasing it.